Wonderful Weekends

A cookbook of menus and their recipes designed for easy, elegant entertaining

Louise Tennent Smith

Wonderful Weekends
Louise Tennent Smith
Copyright 2005
All rights reserved.

ISBN 0-932281-45-1

Cover painting and design by Don Coker

Quill Publications
P.O. Box 8193
Columbus, GA 31908

Foreword

Weekend guests are a delight.

They cover a wide range of types—from comfortable down-home folks to elegant world travelers who've experienced the best. From gatherings of the clan to just-for-fun weekends with friends.

Whatever the occasion, when weekend guests are in the offing, hosts are on stage for three days or so. Even those who can pull off elegant dinners for twelve with no worry blanch at the thought of these encore performances. It may not be quite the equivalent of moving an army and its rations, but the logistics of feeding houseguests for a weekend does require thoughtful planning.

I've found that looking at the weekend as a whole is the best way to plan meals for guests. On the night guests arrive, it seems courteous to provide a good meal at home, with a main course that can be held. And since there is ample prep time, dishes for that meal can take longer to prepare. After that, dishes that can be prepared in advance or quickly are best. On the day guests depart, I think a special brunch is a great send-off.

With these "bookend" meals forming a beginning and an end to the weekend, it becomes easier to see the pattern of the other food to be planned. Think seasonal meals. It doesn't work well to serve a favorite summer-at-the-beach meal in autumn in the mountains. What does work well is using foods of the season to add pleasure to the weekend.

There should be food for nibbling as well—I favor the full cookie jar.

Here are menus and recipes from a lifelong collection. I am not always sure of the source, but have given sources and named names of the donors whenever I could recollect one or the other.

Please dip into this little book for ideas, menus and recipes to make wonderful weekends for you and your guests.

Louise Tennent Smith

Acknowledgments

In the winter of 2000, LYNN WILLOUGHBY and I decided to write a cookbook. Lynn and I fooled around with ideas in fits and starts whenever our disparate schedules would allow, before finally hitting upon the idea of a menu cookbook By the winter of 2004, the pressures of other work and a new direction for her intuitive talent brought Lynn's involvement to a standstill. It was time to fish or cut bait. Lynn decided to cut bait, and I decided to finish the book. Generously, she said, "Take whatever recipes of mine you want and make them yours." Many of the good recipes for baked goods in the book are hers. Thanks especially, Lynn, for the scone recipes and the torta, and for cheering me on all the way.

Thanks also to my niece KATIE BOGLE for the recipes in the section entitled "Katie's Cookie Jar." A great cook, she developed these recipes and cooked them for her happy guests at High Mountain Lodge, a ski resort she owned and operated for a number of years in Colorado.

Thanks to LAURETTE ROSENSTRAUCH for gentle suggestions, and to ALICE ROBERTSON for careful editing and to DON COKER for the handsome cover design.

To RUBYE GOODLETT and JASON McDURMONT of Quill Publications, thanks for patiently providing guidance, and loving attention to the onerous details of publishing a cookbook.

Finally, thanks to friends who gave cherished recipes to me to use, and a tip of the hat to other long-suffering friends, who innocently served as guinea pigs for recipes I tried out on them. That is, all were innocent except Clason Kyle, that witty non-cook, who, invited for dinner and bridge one evening, said "Louise, I just don't think I'm up for one of your experiments. Could I take us to the club for dinner and then come back to your house for bridge?"

"You betcha," I said. It was a lovely evening.

Table of Contents

Foreword 3

Acknowledgments 4

Early Spring 7

Late Spring 21

Early Summer 37

Late Summer 53

Early Fall 71

Late Fall 87

Early Winter 107

Late Winter 127

Katie Bogle's Cookie Jar 143

Index 153

Early Spring

Friday Dinner

Cocktails
*Broccoli & Mushrooms en Croute**

Roast Lamb a la Grecque
*Red Rice Salad**
*Squash Casserole**
Warm Pita
Red Wine
*Summer Pudding**

Saturday Breakfast

Orange Juice
*Peach Upside-Down French Toast**
Bacon
Coffee

Saturday Lunch

*Exotic Shrimp Salad**
English Peas
Crackers
Iced Tea

Saturday Dinner

Cocktails
*Jalapeño Bites**

Zapped Fillet of Flounder
Pan Roasted Asparagus
*Tomato Aspic**
Rolls
*No-Fuss Lemon Pie**
Coffee

Sunday Brunch

*Ricotta Blintz Casserole**
Sugared Strawberries
Brown 'n' Serve Sausages
Coffee

Weekend Nibbles — choose a selection from Katie's Cookie Jar.

*Denotes recipe which can be prepared in whole or in part in advance.

This dish is a combination of recipes from two Junior League cookbooks: One from Charleston, and the other from San Francisco. The filling and the bread bowl can be made ahead of time, and at the last minute, assembled and baked.

BROCCOLI AND MUSHROOMS EN CROUTE

1 round loaf of bread, unsliced
1 medium onion, minced
1/2 pound fresh mushrooms, chopped coarsely
1/2 cup butter
1 can mushroom soup, undiluted
20 ounce package frozen chopped broccoli, defrosted and drained
5-ounce jar Old English cheese spread
Tabasco sauce, to taste
1 tablespoon lemon juice
1 teaspoon Worcestershire sauce, or to taste

Preheat oven to 350 degrees.

Saute onion and mushrooms in butter over low heat until soft. Stir in remaining ingredients, and continue to stir over low heat until cheese melts.*

Slice off top of bread and reserve. Pull out the soft interior of the loaf to make a container for the dip. Spoon the broccoli mixture into it, replace the top and wrap the loaf in foil. Heat in oven for 15 to 20 minutes, or until hot. Serve with corn chips.

Serves 12.

*At this point, you can refrigerate the filling. If you do, add a few minutes to the heating time.

My former brother-in-law Bob Sellas was of Greek descent, and always cooked the lamb himself, stating that it was too important a dish to leave to women. I wheedled this recipe from him, and think women cook it just fine.

ROAST LAMB A LA GRECQUE

4 to 6 pound leg of lamb (try to get New Zealand lamb)
3 garlic cloves, slivered
1 tablespoon EACH salt, pepper and oregano
1 teaspoon thyme
Juice of two lemons
3 cups boiling water

Preheat oven to 425 degrees.

Skin the lamb, slice 1-inch deep holes over the surface and insert the garlic slivers.

Mix together the seasonings and rub over the entire surface of the lamb. Roast uncovered for 1/2 hour. Reduce heat to 350 degrees and roast 1 1/2 hours longer, or until the internal temperature reaches desired doneness (130-135 degrees for medium rare, 140-150 degrees for medium—please don't roast too long!)

During the last half hour of roasting, baste with lemon juice mixed into the boiling water. This last step is crucial for a succulent roast.

Remove from oven and let rest for 15 to 20 minutes before carving.

COOK'S NOTE: If I have any of the roast remaining, which is rare, I chop the remainder and freeze it. Later, it makes a delicious lamb curry.

Red Rice Salad

2 cups water
6-ounce can tomato paste
1 cup raw long grain rice
1 cup chopped onion
1/2 cup chopped green pepper
3/4 teaspoon salt
1/2 cup French dressing, (See page 112 for recipe)
Lemon juice to taste

Place water in a medium saucepan; bring to a boil and stir in tomato paste and rice.

Reduce heat and simmer 15 to 20 minutes or until rice is tender. Cool rice.

Combine cooled rice with green pepper, onion and French dressing. Add lemon juice.

Chill 3 to 4 hours.

Serves 6 to 8.

A squash casserole recipe appears in every cook's collection, but this version is especially nice, since it does not call for cooking the vegetables before putting the casserole together. The shredded carrots, by the way, are added for color but are not essential to the dish.

Squash Casserole

2 pounds yellow squash, sliced thin into rounds
1/2 cup chopped onion
1 can condensed cream of chicken soup
1 cup sour cream
1 cup shredded carrots, optional
Salt and pepper to taste
8-ounce package herb-seasoned stuffing mix
1/2 cup melted butter

Combine all ingredients except stuffing mix and butter in a mixing bowl.

Mix stuffing and butter in another bowl. Sprinkle 1/3 stuffing mixture into a casserole dish, place 1/2 squash mixture on top, repeat. Cover with remainder of the stuffing mix.

Bake at 350 degrees for 50 minutes.

Serves 6.

This superb dessert was once one of the joys of summer, but thanks to frozen fruits, it now can be served the year around. The technique for this version came from "Cook's Illustrated" magazine.

SUMMER PUDDING

8 slices good quality white bread with a dense texture
1 1/2 cups halved hulled fresh strawberries
1 1/2 cups EACH frozen unsweetened raspberries, blueberries and blackberries, unthawed
1/2 cup sugar
1/4 cup cranberry juice
Sweetened whipped cream

Use stale bread or bake the slices in a 200 degree oven for about 45 minutes. Trim crusts.

Heat berries, sugar and juice in a large saucepan over low heat just until berries thaw and sugar dissolves. Remove from heat and cool.

Grease a 9-x-5-inch loaf pan and line it with plastic wrap, extending the wrap well beyond the sides of the pan. Cut bread slices to fit snugly within the pan; set aside.

Place loaf pan on a rimmed baking sheet. With slotted spoon, place about 2 cups of the berries in the bottom of the pan. Lightly press a layer of bread slices into the fruit. Repeat this fruit and bread layering twice more. Top with the remaining juices, cover loosely with plastic wrap, weigh with a second cookie sheet and several cans. Refrigerate overnight.

To serve, unfold plastic wrap and invert pan onto a serving platter. Lift off the pan, remove plastic wrap lining, slice and serve with whipped cream.

Serves 6 to 8.

COOK'S NOTE: You can vary the combination of berries to your taste, but be sure to have a total of 6 cups of fruit..

This breakfast dish was a specialty of mine at Miss Weese's Bed & Breakfast. It will serve 4 as a main breakfast dish with bacon or sausage, or 6 if served with scrambled eggs, muffins, etc.

PEACH UPSIDE-DOWN FRENCH TOAST

8 ounce loaf French bread
4 eggs
1/2 cup milk
1/4 teaspoon baking powder
1 teaspoon almond extract
4 cups sliced peaches, fresh or frozen (not defrosted)
1/2 cup sugar
1 teaspoon nutmeg
1 teaspoon cornstarch
2 tablespoons melted butter

Slice the bread diagonally into 10 to 14 slices about 3/4-inch thick and place on a rimmed baking sheet. Whisk together the eggs, milk, baking powder and extract; slowly pour over the bread, turning bread to coat it completely. Cover with plastic wrap and refrigerate overnight.

Next morning, preheat oven to 450 degrees.

Butter a 9-x-13-inch baking dish. Place peaches in dish. Stir together the sugar, nutmeg and cornstarch and sprinkle over the peaches, stirring a little to coat. Place bread, wettest side up, over fruit, wedging it in tightly. Brush with melted butter.

Bake in center of oven 20 to 25 minutes, or until toast is golden brown and sauce bubbles around the sides. Remove from oven and let rest 5 minutes before serving. Lift toast onto plates, spooning sauce over the top.

Serves 4 to 6.

Andy Anderson was for many years the respected Manager of the Columbus Symphony Orchestra. As well as loving music, he loved good food, and was an excellent cook. This is his recipe for an exotic shrimp salad.

SHRIMP SALAD

2 pounds shrimp, cooked and shelled
1 cup sliced water chestnuts
1/4 cup minced green onions, white part only
1/4 cup minced celery
1 cup mayonnaise
2 teaspoons curry powder
2 tablespoons soy sauce
Lettuce
Litchi nuts and toasted slivered almonds for garnish.

Combine first seven ingredients, toss well. Pile into nests of lettuce. Garnish with canned litchi nuts and almonds.

Serves 6.

Our neighbor Ron Self gives a New Year's Day party every year. This zesty and easy recipe is a hit every time.

JALAPEÑO BITES

12-ounce jar sliced jalapeño peppers, rinsed and drained
6 eggs, beaten
2 cups grated sharp cheddar cheese

Preheat oven to 350 degrees.

Spray a 9-x-13-inch pan with cooking spray.
Scatter peppers in bottom of pan. Scatter cheese over peppers and pour egg mixture carefully over all. Bake 35 to 40 minutes. Slice into squares and serve warm or at room temperature. Serves 6 to 8.

❄ ❄ ❄

This recipe is so good you'll find it hard to believe it's so easy. It can be zapped at the last minute, is fool proof, and makes its own sauce!

ZAPPED FILLET OF FLOUNDER

Flounder or sole fillets, one for each person
Sour cream
Dill Weed
Parmesan cheese

Arrange fish fillets in one layer on a microwave-safe pan. Cover them with sour cream, and sprinkle generously with dill weed and freshly grated Parmesan cheese (not the kind in those green cartons!)

Zap on high until flaky, about 4 to 7 minutes. Let rest 1 or 2 minutes before serving.

Pan Roasted Asparagus

2 pounds fresh asparagus, trimmed
2 to 3 tablespoons olive oil, divided use
Salt and freshly ground pepper to taste
2 tablespoons lemon juice
1 tablespoon orange juice

Place the asparagus in a single layer in a large, nonstick skillet and drizzle with one tablespoon of the olive oil. Shake pan to coat the asparagus and place over medium heat.
Cook, shaking the pan every few minutes to brown evenly. Lower the heat and continue cooking until tender, 10 to 15 minutes, depending on the size of the asparagus.

Season with salt and pepper. Drizzle with remaining olive oil.

Combine juices, drizzle over asparagus and serve immediately.

Serves 4.

This recipe has been a favorite for years. I use plain V-8 juice, but if you prefer it spicier try the spicy version, or add Tabasco.

Tomato Aspic

32 ounces V-8 juice
4 envelopes plain gelatin
Seasonings to taste: Onion juice, lemon juice, salt, pepper, etc.

Dissolve gelatin in 2 cups of the juice. Heat the rest of the juice to boiling. Stir in gelatin mix.

Season to taste, pour into a ring mold and refrigerate until set.

Makes one ring mold.

I always keep two packages of Minute Maid's frozen lemon juice on hand—one in the refrigerator and one in the freezer. One day, after reading the recipe on the box, I tried it out on my dinner guests. It was declared a winner.

NO-FUSS LEMON PIE

3 large eggs
1/2 bottle Minute Maid frozen lemon juice, defrosted
1 1/4 cups sugar
1/4 cup melted butter
1 unbaked pie shell
Sweetened whipped cream, optional

Preheat oven to 350 degrees.

Combine first 3 ingredients in a blender; blend 3 minutes, or until smooth. Add butter, blend 30 seconds. Pour into pastry shell. Bake 30 to 35 minutes. Top with whipped cream if desired.

Serves 6.

This delicious recipe is a holiday favorite at Joe and Kathy Alexander's home. We didn't see why one could not enjoy it year-round, and so we do. It can be prepared the night before and cooked in the morning.

RICOTTA BLINTZ CASSEROLE

Filling:
    2 pounds ricotta cheese
    2 eggs
    1/4 cup sugar
    1/8 teaspoon salt
    1/4 cup lemon juice
    8 ounces cream cheese, softened

Place ingredients in mixer and blend well. Set aside.

Batter:
    1/2 pound butter, melted
    1/2 cup sugar
    2 eggs
    1 cup sifted flour
    3 teaspoons baking powder
    1/8 teaspoon salt
    1/4 cup milk
    1 teaspoon vanilla

Mix batter ingredients by hand and spoon half of it in the bottom of a greased 3-quart round casserole dish. Carefully spread all of filling on top. Spoon remaining batter over filling.

Bake at 300 degrees for 1 1/2 hours. (if prepared the night before and refrigerated, start in a cool oven and allow 10-15 minutes extra baking time.) Top with foil to prevent overbrowning for last half hour if needed.

Serves 8.

Late Spring

Friday Dinner

Cocktails
*Mushroom Caviar**

*Shrimp Curry — Rice**
Curry Accompaniments
Beer
*Dark Chocolate Torta**
Coffee

Saturday Breakfast

Baked Swiss Eggs
Kiwi Slices
Croissants and Jam
Coffee

Saturday Lunch

*Cold Cucumber Soup**
Tortilla Rolls
Sparkling Mineral Water

Saturday Dinner

Cocktails
Yum-Yum Vidalias*

Chicken Picante
Packaged Herb Rice
Broccoli Salad*
Strawberry Tart*
Iced Tea

Sunday Brunch

Golden Coins*
Link Sausages
Applesauce
Cheddar Biscuits*
Coffee

Weekend Nibbles — choose a selection from Katie's Cookie Jar.

*Denotes recipe which can be prepared in whole or in part in advance.

This recipe is one from a company that sells spices—again proving that often the best recipes come from the manufacturers of food products. After all, they have those huge testing kitchens, and all those people working to perfect ways of using the product!

Mushroom Caviar

3 tablespoons olive oil
1/2 pound mushrooms, chopped coarsely
1/3 cup chopped onion
1 1/2 teaspoons lemon juice
1/2 teaspoon salt
1/8 teaspoon garlic powder
Dash cayenne pepper
2 teaspoons dried dill weed
1/2 cup sour cream

Saute onion and mushrooms in oil until onions are soft.
Transfer to mixing bowl and stir in remaining ingredients.
Refrigerate.
Serve cold or at room temperature, with crackers.

Serves 4 to 6.

Shrimp Curry

2 1/2 pounds cleaned raw shrimp
1/2 cup butter
2 to 3 tablespoons curry powder
1 1/4 cup chopped onion
1 1/2 cups peeled and diced apple
2 chicken bouillon cubes dissolved in 2 cups hot water
2 tablespoons cornstarch dissolved in 1/4 cup cold water
1 cup evaporated milk, undiluted
1 teaspoon lemon juice, or to taste

Melt butter in extra large skillet. Add the curry, chopped apple and onion. Add dissolved bouillon cubes and water. Simmer, stirring occasionally, for 10 minutes.

Stir cornstarch mixture into skillet and stir until thickened. Add the cleaned shrimp and the milk. Mix well and simmer covered for ten minutes.*

Add lemon juice, correct the seasoning and serve over white rice with some of the condiments listed on the next page.

Serves 6.

*At this point, you may either refrigerate the mixture for a day or two, or freeze. Reheat gradually over low heat.

In the colonial Dutch East Indies, serving boys circled the dining table bearing dishes of condiments for the curry, the number of servers matching the number of accompaniments. While it may be difficult to round up ten children these days, your guests will still enjoy choosing among an array of condiments to customize their own plates of curry.

Accompaniments for a Ten-Boy Curry

Chutney
Mandarin oranges
Nuts: chopped peanuts or cashews or whole almonds
Chopped olives, ripe or green
Chopped crisp bacon
Raisins
Toasted Coconut
Crystallized ginger, minced
Chopped bananas
Small pickled onions

This flourless chocolate cake is elegant yet easy to prepare. It is inspired by Roxanne Gold's recipe in "Cooking 1-2-3."

DARK CHOCOLATE TORTA

2 cups good quality semisweet chocolate chips
3/4 cup good quality bittersweet chocolate chips
10 tablespoons butter, cut into chunks
6 large eggs
For garnish, whipped cream and fresh raspberries, optional

Preheat oven to 375 degrees.

Coat the sides of an 8 1/2-inch spring form pan with nonstick cooking spray. Cut parchment paper to fit the bottom.

Stirring frequently, melt the chocolate and butter in a double boiler over (but not touching) simmering water.

Meanwhile, whisk eggs with a pinch of salt in the bowl of an electric mixer until tripled in volume, about 8 minutes. Fold chocolate mixture into eggs until completely incorporated.

Pour batter into prepared pan and bake for 20 minutes. The center should still be a little soft. Cool for at least 30 minutes before cutting, or refrigerate the cake for up to 2 days, then let sit at room temperature for about an hour before serving.

This cake is very rich, and you need only serve small slices. Garnish, if desired, with whipped cream and a few fresh raspberries.

Serves 8 to 10.

This breakfast dish is great for carb-watchers, and was inspired by a recipe in The Carbohydrate Addict's Cookbook *by the Doctors Richard and Rachael Heller.*

BAKED SWISS EGGS

For each person, you will need

1 thin slice Swiss cheese, such as Sargento's Deli Slices
1 egg
Nutmeg and salt to taste
1 or 2 tablespoons half-and-half
Freshly grated Parmesan cheese

Preheat oven to 350 degrees.

Spray a ramekin with vegetable oil. Place a slice of the cheese inside, break an egg over it, sprinkle with salt and nutmeg. Carefully pour in the cream. Top with a generous sprinkle of the Parmesan.

Bake for 12 minutes.

I invited a couple of newspaper people to lunch one day, and served this cold soup. One of them began to describe a scene (I believe it was in Oklahoma) following a severe tornado. "They had tents up to feed the homeless," he said, "and even THEY had hot soup to eat."

Oh, well. Many men don't appreciate cold soup.

COLD CUCUMBER SOUP

2 to 3 cucumbers, peeled, seeded and cut into chunks
1 quart buttermilk
4 tablespoons chopped scallions OR 1 onion, chopped
Salt and pepper to taste
1/4 cup chopped dill weed
Thin slices of radish for garnish, optional

Place cucumbers in blender or food processor with a cup of the buttermilk. Add scallions, salt, pepper and dill. Process until smooth. Stir in remaining buttermilk, mixing thoroughly. Refrigerate.

When well chilled, taste for seasoning, and garnish with radish slices, if desired.

Serves 6.

These are fun. Each person rolls his own, choosing ingredients from an array you have provided. I prefer the flavored tortillas if you can find them, in particular the tomato-herb. They are prettier, and have more flavor.

Tortilla Rolls

Flour tortillas
Mayonnaise
Mustard
Spicy hummus
Sliced roast beef
Sliced turkey
Cold cuts
Cheeses: Swiss, cheddar, feta, etc.
Ripe olives and green olives
Pickles
Shredded lettuce

Place a large selection of meat and cheeses on platters, and offer pots of mustard, hummus and mayonnaise, dishes of pickles and olives.

Each person spreads his tortilla with preferred condiments, meats and cheese (for instance, turkey and Swiss cheese with mustard, mayonnaise and sweet Gherkins) rolls it up and slices it slantwise into two pieces.

Norman Rothschild was an art lover, philanthropist and cook. He won a recipe contest with this recipe.

Yum-Yum Vidalias

4 or 5 medium Vidalia onions, sliced very thin
2 cups water
1 cup sugar
1/2 cup cider vinegar
1/2 cup mayonnaise
1 teaspoon celery salt
1 teaspoon celery seed

Soak the onion slices for 6 hours or overnight in the refrigerator in a mixture of the water, sugar and vinegar. Drain well, pressing liquid out of the onions. Mix together the mayonnaise, celery salt and celery seed, then stir into the onions. Chill well.

Put in a pretty glass bowl, and serve with melba toast rounds or crackers.

Serves 12.

This chicken dish won a prize at the national chicken cooking contest a few years back. This is the perfect recipe: Guests always love it, it is not laden with fat, it looks good and it's easy to do.

CHICKEN PICANTE

4 boneless, skinless chicken breast halves
1/2 cup medium chunky taco sauce
1/4 cup Dijon mustard
2 tablespoons fresh lime juice
2 tablespoons butter
6 tablespoons plain yogurt
1 lime, peeled and sliced

In a large bowl, mix taco sauce, mustard and lime juice. Add chicken and turn to coat. Marinate for at least 30 minutes.

Melt butter over medium heat until foamy. Remove chicken from marinate, reserving liquid, and cook in butter about 10 minutes per side. Add reserved marinade and cook about 5 more minutes, or until fork can be inserted with ease. Marinade should be slightly reduced and beginning to glaze. Remove chicken to serving plate.

Raise heat to high, boil marinade 1 minute and pour over chicken. Place a heaping tablespoon of yogurt on each piece of chicken. Top with a slice of lime.

Serves 4.

This bright salad can be served at room temperature, or refrigerated until serving time. If you plan to hold it for several hours, or all day, add the crumbled bacon just before serving. I often use Baco bits instead of bacon.

BROCCOLI SALAD

1 cup mayonnaise
2 tablespoons sugar
2 tablespoons red wine vinegar
1 pound fresh broccoli florets, chopped
5 bacon slices, cooked and crumbled
1/2 cup raisins
1/4 cup chopped onion

Stir together the first 3 ingredients in a large bowl. Add the broccoli and remaining ingredients and toss well. Refrigerate until serving time.

Serves 8.

Don't tell anyone this tart is healthy, and they'll never know. It tastes just like a custard pie, but without the eggs and cream, and it's a cinch to make. Lynn adapted the recipe from "Vegetarian Times."

Strawberry "Custard" Tart

1 pie crust
1 1/2 cups silken tofu, drained in colander for about 10 minutes
1/2 cup sugar
1 tablespoon melted butter
1 teaspoon vanilla
1/4 teaspoon almond extract
1 teaspoon dark rum, divided use
2 cups fresh strawberries, stems removed
1/2 cup fruit-sweetened strawberry preserves

Bake crust until lightly browned; cool.

In food processor or blender, combine tofu, butter, sugar, extracts and half the rum. Process until well blended, about 30 seconds. Pour into cooled crust and bake at 350 degrees until set, about 25 minutes, wrapping foil around crust edges to prevent over-browning. Cool.

Arrange strawberries over custard, pointed side up, covering surface completely.

Puree preserves with remaining rum. Brush over strawberries. Chill for at least an hour before serving.

Serves 6.

I like to bake an oven full of sweet potatoes at a time, freezing them in their skins (no need to wrap) for later use. Using some of your frozen sweets for this dish makes it an almost instant delight.

Golden Coins

1 frozen sweet potato for 2 guests
Butter
Salt
Sugar
Grated nutmeg
Maple syrup

Take out of the freezer the number of sweet potatoes you will need and allow to sit at room temperature until they are sliceable—about 5 minutes. Peel and slice into 3/4-inch rounds.

Melt butter in a large frying pan. Place as many potato rounds as you can fit into the pan in a single layer. When browned on the bottom, about 3 minutes, turn them over and sprinkle the browned side with salt, sugar and nutmeg to taste. When the second side is browned, remove to an ovenproof plate to keep warm while you repeat with the remaining rounds.

Drizzle with maple syrup and serve hot.

These biscuits are the most popular breakfast bread Lynn Willoughby serves at her summer house near Highlands. They are absolutely wonderful stuffed with ham. She likes using half butter and half shortening because of the flavor butter adds, but you can use shortening alone if you wish. Serve them hot or not—they are the best cold biscuits you'll ever eat, and they freeze well.

CHEDDAR BISCUITS

2 cups self-rising flour
1/2 teaspoon salt
2 tablespoons shortening, cut into 1/4-inch pieces
2 tablespoons butter, cut into 1/4-inch pieces
1 1/2 cups grated sharp cheddar cheese
3/4 cup buttermilk, light cream OR yogurt

Preheat oven to 400 degrees.

In a medium bowl mix together flour and salt. Using a pastry cutter or your fingers, cut the butter and/or shortening until the mixture resembles coarse meal. Or, using the food processor, process for about 30 seconds. Mix in the grated cheese.

In mixing bowl, make a well in the dry ingredients and pour in the buttermilk and stir quickly until the dough forms a ball, adding a bit more liquid if there is excess flour remaining. Turn onto a flour-dusted surface and knead twice.

Pat or roll the dough to 3/4-inch thickness. Cut the biscuits, using a 1 3/4 inch cutter. Place biscuits on an ungreased baking sheet, 3 inches apart if you like crusty sides, or 1/2 inch apart if you like softer biscuits.

Bake about 12 minutes, until slightly browned.

Makes 10 to 12 biscuits.

Early Summer

Friday Dinner

Cocktails
Chicken Liver Paté *

Oven Barbecued Beef Brisket*
Oven Roasted Vegetable Salad*
Rolls
Peach Cobbler
Iced Tea

Saturday Breakfast

Vegetable Juice
Baked Blueberry French Toast
Bacon
Coffee

Saturday Lunch

Curried Chicken Salad in Avocado Shells*
Toasted Saltines
Ginger Lemonade*

Saturday Dinner

Cocktails
*Crock o' Cheese**

Grilled Steaks
Vidalia Onion Casserole
Corn on the Cob
Garlic Bread
*Ice Cream Pie**
Iced Tea

Sunday Brunch

*Fresh Fruit Burton**
Tomato Pie
*Marinated Green Beans**
Purchased Sausage Rolls
Coffee

Weekend Nibbles — choose a selection from Katie's Cookie Jar.

*Denotes recipe which can be prepared in whole or in part in advance.

Chicken Liver Paté

1 pound chicken livers
8 tablespoons butter
2 tablespoons Armagnac OR Cognac
3 tablespoons Port, Madeira OR Sherry
1 clove garlic, finely minced
1 1/2 teaspoons salt
Freshly ground pepper to taste
Four Spices to taste (recipe on following page)

Pick over livers, removing any fat, green particles, or extraneous bits. Melt 2 tablespoons butter in a sauté pan; cook livers 2 to 3 minutes until they stiffen but are still slightly pink inside. Put the livers in a food processor or blender and process to a fine paste.

Add Armagnac or Cognac to the sauté pan and cook 1 minute; add the wine and cook another minute, scraping up any residue from the livers. Add this to the food processor with the remaining ingredients, including the remaining butter, and process briefly to mix well. Taste for seasoning and add the spices as needed.

Scrape the mixture into a serving dish and refrigerate until firm, about 2 hours.

Serve with toast.

COOK'S NOTE: Put the paté in a jar covered with oil to seal it, and it will keep 3 weeks in the refrigerator.

Four Spices

Mix together:
2 teaspoons ground pepper, preferably white
1/4 teaspoon ground cloves
1/4 teaspoon ground ginger
1/4 teaspoon ground nutmeg

Store in a tightly closed jar.

SUBSTITUTIONS

Self-Rising flour: For 1 cup self-rising flour, substitute 1 cup sifted all-purpose flour plus 1 1/2 teaspoons baking powder and 1/2 teaspoon salt.

Buttermilk or sour milk: 1 tablespoon vinegar or lemon juice, plus enough sweet milk to make one cup. Let stand 5 minutes.

Garlic: For 1 medium clove garlic, use 1/8 teaspoon garlic powder or 3/4 teaspoon garlic salt. Or keep a jar of purchased minced garlic in the refrigerator.

Lemon peel: For 1 teaspoon lemon peel, use 1/2 teaspoon lemon extract.

Onion: 1 small onion equals 1 teaspoon onion powder or 1 teaspoon minced dry onion.

Bread crumbs: 3/4 cup cracker crumbs equals 1 cup bread crumbs.

Sour cream: 1 cup plain yogurt or 7/8 cup sour milk plus 1/3 cup butter.

Oven Barbecued Beef Brisket

3 to 4 pound beef brisket
Liquid Smoke
Garlic salt
Celery salt
2 large yellow onions, sliced
1 bottle good quality barbecue sauce

Rub meat with Liquid Smoke, then sprinkle with garlic and celery salts. Place half the onion slices on aluminum foil large enough to fold over and seal the meat. Put meat on foil, cover with remaining onion slices and seal foil, double folding the ends.

Place meat in a large pan and roast in a preheated 350 degree oven for 30 minutes. Reduce heat to 250 degrees and roast for 3 hours longer, or until meat is fork tender.

Remove from oven, and when cool enough to handle, slice across the grain. Rewrap and refrigerate until the next day.

Next day, place brisket slices in a pan, cover with the barbecue sauce and heat in oven.

Serves 6 to 8.

Roasted Vegetable Salad

1 3/4 pounds red new potatoes
2 tablespoons olive oil, divided
1 1/2 cups fresh green beans, cut into 2-inch pieces
1 cup carrots cut in thin diagonal pieces
1 red onion, cut into wedges
3 tablespoons balsamic vinegar
2 tablespoons water
1/2 teaspoon salt
1/4 teaspoon pepper

Cut potatoes into eighths, toss with half the oil. Place on a jelly roll pan and bake at 450 degrees for 15 minutes. Toss remaining vegetables with remaining oil; add to baking pan; stir; continue baking 15 minutes more, or until vegetables are tender.

Meanwhile, in bowl, stir together vinegar, water and seasonings. When vegetables are done, add to bowl and toss well.

Serve chilled or at room temperature.

Serves 6.

Most cooks have a recipe similar to this one for peach cobbler. (If you haven't, you need one!) The version that follows has more fruit and less butter than many, and the nutmeg is a good addition to this classic Southern dessert.

PEACH COBBLER

3 cups sliced peaches, mixed with 1/4 cup sugar
2 teaspoons lemon juice
1/2 cup butter
3/4 cup all-purpose flour
2 teaspoons baking powder
3/4 cup sugar
1/4 teaspoon salt
3/4 cup milk
Dash or two of nutmeg

Sprinkle lemon juice over sugared peaches and set aside.

Preheat oven to 350 degrees.

Melt butter in microwave in the bottom of a deep Pyrex or ceramic baking dish.

Make a batter of the remaining ingredients, except nutmeg, and pour (DO NOT STIR) over the melted butter. Pour peaches on top of batter. Again, DO NOT STIR. Sprinkle nutmeg on top.

Bake until crust is light brown and puffy, approximately 45 to 50 minutes. Serve warm with a dollop of vanilla ice cream.

Serves 6 to 8.

I plucked this recipe in Nova Scotia, where the blueberries grow and grow and grow. It's a guaranteed crowd pleaser.

BAKED BLUEBERRY FRENCH TOAST

10 thick slices of white bread
8 ounces cream cheese, softened to room temperature
1 pint blueberries
6 eggs
2 cups half-and-half
2 tablespoons maple syrup
2 teaspoons vanilla
Powdered sugar

Preheat oven to 400 degrees.

Arrange bread slices so they fit into a greased jelly roll baking sheet. Spread softened cream cheese over the bread. Press blueberries into the cream cheese.

Beat together the eggs, cream, syrup and vanilla. Gently pour over the bread. Bake for 15 to 20 minutes, or until browned on top and firm to the touch.

Sprinkle with confectioners sugar and serve with warm maple syrup.

Serves 8 to 10.

This is a pleasant change from the ordinary, and is beautiful served in avocado halves.

CURRIED CHICKEN SALAD

4 chicken breast halves, steamed just until cooked through
1 to 2 teaspoons curry powder
1/2 teaspoon salt
Pepper to taste
1 tablespoon lemon juice
1 cup diced cantaloupe
1 cup seedless grapes
1/2 cup walnut pieces
2 tablespoons minced candied ginger
1/4 cup sour cream OR yogurt
1/2 cup mayonnaise
3 unskinned avocados, halved

Bone and skin breasts as soon as they are cool enough to handle. Cut into 1-inch cubes and toss with curry powder, salt, pepper and lemon juice. Refrigerate until cold. Add remaining ingredients, and serve in avocado halves on lettuce.

Serves 6.

Sally Spencer's recipe — the perfect drink for a hot summer day.

GINGER LEMONADE

6 cups water, divided use
1 1/4 cups sugar
1/4 cup grated, peeled fresh ginger
1 1/2 cups fresh lemon juice

Combine 1 cup water, the sugar and the ginger in a small saucepan and boil for 1 minute, stirring occasionally to dissolve sugar. Remove from heat and allow to cool.

Strain the ginger syrup into a pitcher, discarding solids. Add 5 cups cold water and the lemon juice and stir. Refrigerate until serving time.

Serves 6.

When Mother made this dish, the family knew it was a party. You'll note the recipe says "squish together." Of course your hands will be clean, but the best way to make this is to use your fingers. This improves with age.

CROCK O'CHEESE

8 ounces cream cheese
1 stick butter
4 ounces Roquefort cheese (don't skimp!)
2 tablespoons grated onion
2 teaspoons Worcestershire sauce, or to taste

Soften butter and cheese. Squish together with onion and Worcestershire. Serve in a crock, with wheat crackers.

Serves 8 to 10.

❈ ❈ ❈

This is easy — no boiling water, corn that is faintly crisp to the bite — but be sure to wear oven gloves when shucking the corn!

CORN ON THE COB

Put one ear of unshucked corn (silks and all) for each person, 2 or 3 at the time in the microwave and zap on high 2 minutes per ear.

Remove from oven, shuck, and roll each ear on a stick of butter. Serve immediately, allowing each diner to salt and pepper.

Jean Hull, a college classmate, won a James Beard cooking contest out on the West Coast with this recipe. She used the Walla Walla sweet onion. Naturally, we changed that to our famous Georgia sweet Vidalia. Don't be alarmed at the amount of onion listed—7 1/2 cups is correct.

VIDALIA ONION CASSEROLE

7 1/2 cups Vidalia onions, chopped
4 tablespoons butter
1/2 cup raw rice
5 cups boiling water, salted
3/4 cup grated Swiss cheese
2/3 cup half-and-half

Saute onions in butter.

Cook rice in salted water for 5 minutes, drain and mix with onion. Add cheese and cream.

Bake, covered, at 350 degrees for 1 hour.

Serves 6 to 8.

There are many recipes for ice cream pie. Basically, one uses a crumb crust of graham crackers, chocolate wafers or Oreos. It may be purchased ready made or made at home. Today you can even buy the crumbs in a box, ready crushed. Into this crust, one places softened ice cream—one flavor, or layered, or two swirled together. After freezing the whole, the pie can be served with a sauce that complements the ice cream. It's fun to do, and you can be creative here. Following is one example of an ice cream pie.

ICE CREAM PIE

1 1/4 cups chocolate wafer crumbs
3 tablespoons sugar
1/3 cup melted butter or margarine
1 quart orange sherbet, softened
Raspberry sauce, recipe follows
Fresh raspberries for garnish, optional

Mix first three ingredients together. With fingers, press into bottom and up the sides of a pie plate. Chill.

Spread softened sherbet into the chilled pie shell; wrap and freeze. Serve with raspberry sauce. Garnish with raspberries. Serves 6.

RASPBERRY SAUCE

8 ounces frozen raspberries
3 tablespoons sugar
1 teaspoon cornstarch, dissolved in 2 tablespoons water.

Heat fruit and sugar until berries are defrosted and sugar dissolved. Press through a sieve to remove seeds. Return to heat and stir in cornstarch solution, stirring constantly until the sauce is clear and begins to thicken. Cool to room temperature or refrigerate.

Summers at Lake Burton were always special. Some of this summer fruit mélange was always kept cool in the refrigerator.

Fresh Fruit Burton

4 or 5 peaches, peeled and sliced
1 1/2 cups fresh blueberries
3/4 cup orange juice

Cover fruit with orange juice and refrigerate.

Feel free to add other summer fruit such as cantaloupe, strawberries or blackberries. Just be sure the fruit is covered by the orange juice.

Serves 4 to 6.

❄ ❄ ❄

Sister Schubert makes good sausage rolls you can buy ready made in the freezer section of the grocery store. Or you can make your own.

Sausage Wraps

2 packs refrigerated crescent rolls
16 cocktail franks (like L'il Smokies)

Unroll dough and separate into triangles. Place a cocktail frank on each triangle and roll up. Bake in a preheated 400 degree oven for 7-9 minutes or until brown.

Makes 16 sausage wraps.

Billy Winn is noted for his writing, and also for this tomato pie. Now that he's shared the recipe, you can be noted also.

TOMATO PIE

1 pie shell, lightly browned
3/4 pound Gruyere, sliced thin or grated
4 or 5 large vine-ripened tomatoes, skinned, sliced, salted and drained
1 tablespoon fresh basil, chopped
2 tablespoons olive oil
2 tablespoons Parmesan cheese

Preheat oven to 350 degrees.
Into pie shell, layer half the cheese, then half the tomatoes. Sprinkle with half the basil and half the oil. Repeat the layer, and top with the Parmesan. Bake for 20 to 30 minutes.

Serves 6.

MARINATED GREEN BEANS

2 pounds tender green beans, ends trimmed and halved
French or Vinaigrette dressing, bottled or homemade

Drop beans into boiling, salted water, a few at a time so that the water continues to boil.

Cook for about 5 minutes, or until beans are crisp-tender. Drain and refresh immediately with cold water.

Turn beans into a glass dish and cover immediately with French dressing. (See page 112) Chill several hours.

Serves 6 to 8.

Late Summer

Friday Dinner

Sangria*
Goat Cheese Tarts*

Never-fail Roast Beef*
Tangy Microwave Cauliflower
Pea Salad*
Rolls
Watermelon
Iced Tea

Saturday Breakfast

Mixed Summer Berries with Yogurt
Lemon Bread*
Sausage Patties
Coffee

Saturday Lunch

Cold Carrot Ginger Soup*
Roast Beef Sandwiches
Iced Mint Tea*

Saturday Dinner

Cocktails
*Jezebel Sauce on Cream Cheese**

Low Country Boil
*Seven Day Slaw**
Hush Puppies
Beer
*Brownies with Peppermint Ice Cream**

Sunday Brunch

Cantaloupe Slices
Simple Cheese Souffle
Sliced Tomatoes with Fresh Basil
Assorted Sweet Rolls

Weekend Nibbles — choose a selection from Katie's Cookie Jar.

*Denotes recipe which can be prepared in whole or in part in advance.

This is a great hot weather drink, and can be made with almost anything you have on hand as long as you start with a bottle of wine and a pitcher of ice. Usually it is made with red wine, but white is good also. Be creative. One summer day I used red wine, Apple Jack and Sprite, garnished with peaches. It disappeared quickly.

SANGRIA

1 bottle wine
1/4 cup brandy or flavored Schnapps
Small bottle soda
1/4 cup sugar, optional
Slices of apple, lemon, orange or peach

Fill a pitcher with ice. Pour in the liquids, sweeten (if desired), stir, garnish with fruit.
Serve over ice in pretty glasses.

Serves 4 to 6.

On a food writer's trip to the Niagara Food and Wine Festival, I attended a class at The Good Earth Cooking School. It was outside, in one of the orchards located in Canada's lovely "table land" east of Toronto. The first words out of owner Nicolette Novak's mouth could serve as my motto: "Cooking should be fun," she said. "For instance, we didn't make these little puff pastry shells, we bought them."

She's right—buy these little delicacies at the store, and fill them with something delicious. At The Good Earth, they were filled with goat cheese, topped with little slices of fresh peach, drizzled with lavender-infused honey. They were delicious, and led me to thinking about another easy Canadian recipe we garnered in Canada—tomato preserves.

This appetizer combines the two.

GOAT CHEESE TARTS WITH TOMATO PRESERVES

15 mini fillo shells (purchased in frozen food section)
4 ounces goat cheese
Tomato preserves, recipe follows on next page.

Defrost tarts, and following directions on package, crisp briefly (3 to 5 minutes) in a preheated 350 degree oven. Place a scant teaspoon of goat cheese in each tart. Top with a dab of the tomato preserves or hot pepper jelly, or a jam of your choice. Serve immediately.

Makes 15 appetizers.

Tomato Preserves

2 cups chopped tomatoes (not seeded, not peeled)
1/2 cup sugar
1 vanilla bean
To taste: lemon juice, Tabasco

Place ingredients in saucepan and cook over medium heat, stirring occasionally, about 30 minutes, or until jam becomes thickened.

Makes about 1 cup.

❇ ❇ ❇

Always work in a clean kitchen, tidying up as you go. It'll make cooking easier, and when you finish, you'll be glad.

The first time you try a new recipe, read it over several times before beginning. Don't improvise until you have cooked it once as is.

Check to be sure you have the ingredients needed before beginning the recipe. It's awful to be in the middle of making a dish and be without a key ingredient.

This recipe is so simple you won't believe it's possible. It is fool proof, and is a perfect entrée for holding over when guests' arrival time is uncertain.

NEVER-FAIL ROAST BEEF

6 pound standing rib roast
Salt, pepper
Herbs of choice

Have the butcher cut away the ribs and tie them back together for easy carving at home, but with the full flavor rendered by the bones.

Allow roast to come to room temperature and stand for 1 hour. Meanwhile, preheat the oven to 400 degrees.

Rub the meat with salt and pepper and any herb you like. Place on broiling pan, rib side down. Turn oven temperature down to 375 degrees and roast for one hour. Turn oven off.

DO NOT OPEN OVEN DOOR!!!

30 to 40 minutes before serving turn oven on again to 375 degrees. Cook for 30 minutes for perfectly rare, 45 minutes for well done.

Serves 6.

I got this recipe many years ago at a cooking school in Miami. In fact, it was so long ago that microwave cooking was fairly new, but I still love the recipe for its ease and taste.

Tangy Microwave Cauliflower

1 medium head cauliflower
2 tablespoons water
1/2 cup mayonnaise
1 teaspoon mustard
1 teaspoon finely chopped onion
1/2 cup shredded cheddar

Place trimmed cauliflower in 1 1/2 quart casserole dish. Add water, cover and microwave on high for 8 minutes.

Combine mayonnaise, mustard and onion; spoon on top of cauliflower; sprinkle with cheese; microwave on roast setting for 1 1/2 to 2 minutes.

Let stand 2 minutes before serving.

Serves 4 to 6.

Elinor Winn serves this pea salad to grateful friends. The recipe makes a lot and can be held in the refrigerator for several days. It's also great to take to a covered-dish dinner.

Pea Salad

2 15-ounce cans small English peas
2 15-ounce cans cut green beans (NOT French cut)
4 stalks celery, chopped fine
1 bell pepper, chopped fine
1 medium onion, chopped fine
4 ounce jar chopped pimento, drained

Mix the above ingredients in a large bowl.

In a saucepan, blend together the following and bring to a boil:

> 1 1/2 cups sugar
> 1 cup cider vinegar
> 1/2 cup vegetable oil

Cover the vegetables with the liquid and chill for 8 to 10 hours before serving.

Serves 10 to 12.

Warning! The lemon intensity of this quick bread makes it highly addictive. If you mix it in a food processor, the step of chopping the nuts is eliminated.

LEMON BREAD

1/2 cup shortening or oil
1 cup sugar
2 eggs
Zest of 1 lemon
1 1/2 cups plain flour
1 1/2 teaspoons baking powder
1/4 teaspoon salt
1/2 cup milk
1 cup chopped pecans, almonds, or other nuts OR 1/2 cup minced crystallized ginger
Juice of 1 lemon mixed with 1/4 cup powdered sugar.

Cream shortening and sugar. Add eggs, one at a time, then lemon zest.

In separate bowl, mix flour baking powder and salt. Add flour mixture to sugar mixture, alternately with milk. Stir in nuts or ginger.

Pour into an 8 1/2-x-4 1/2-inch loaf pan and bake at 350 degrees for 1 hour. Let sit for 10 minutes, then invert pan onto a rack. Pour the sweetened lemon juice over top of loaf and allow to absorb into the bread.

Serves 10 to 12.

COOK'S NOTE: If you zest with a vegetable peeler, you will have to chop the peel. If you treat yourself to a zester (I use a Microplane) you will not.

My long-time best friend, Sarah Ann Bankston Waters of Atlanta (we played in sand piles together, and our mothers were friends, as were our grandmothers) gave me this delicious, and healthy, recipe. I drink it by the glassful, and once dipped into it so often that my hands began to turn yellow.

COLD CARROT GINGER SOUP

1 tablespoon butter
1 large onion, chopped coarsely
1/4 cup fresh ginger, peeled and sliced thin
3 cloves garlic, slivered
7 cups chicken stock
1 cup dry white wine
1 1/2 pounds carrots, peeled and cut into chunks
2 tablespoons fresh or frozen lemon juice
Pinch curry powder, or to taste
Salt and pepper to taste, if desired
Plain yogurt for garnish, optional

Saute onion, ginger and garlic in butter for about 15 minutes. Meanwhile, simmer carrots in chicken stock and wine until tender. Reserving stock, puree carrots in food processor in a little stock. Add onion mixture and puree.

Mix together pureed vegetables with reserved stock. Stir in remaining ingredients. Chill.

Serve with a generous dollop of yogurt if desired.

Serves 6 to 8.

This is so simple, yet so delicious—it's a thirst quenching summer pick-me-up.

Iced Mint Tea

6 cups water
5 Bigelow's Plantation Mint tea bags
3 artificial sweetener packets (or sugar) to taste

Turn burner to medium-high. Place pot with water and tea-bags (paper tags removed and strings tied together) on burner. Do not let water boil, but when bubbles begin to form on sides of the pot, about 12 minutes, remove from heat and let stand 3 minutes. Remove tea bags and stir in sweetener. Chill.

Serve over ice.

4 to 6 servings.

Jezebel Sauce

1.2 ounce can dry mustard
4 ounce jar horseradish
16 ounce jar pineapple preserves
16 ounce jar apple jelly
2 tablespoons coarsely ground black pepper

Make a paste of the first two ingredients. Stir in remaining ingredients until thoroughly mixed. Place over blocks of cream cheese, and serve with crackers.

Makes 1 quart.

Ingredients here are flexible—they can be adjusted to suit the size and tastes of your crowd. For an easy cleanup, serve inside or outside on a table covered with newspapers. Each person peels his own shrimp and throws peelings and corncobs into the center of the table. At meal's end, just roll up the newspaper and throw it in the garbage. It isn't elegant, but it is surely fun!

Low Country Boil

For every six guests use:

- 1 box crab and shrimp boil seasoning—Zatarain's is good
- 1 1/2 pounds Italian sausage (mild or spicy) cut into 2-inch pieces
- 5 or 6 ears of corn, shucked and broken into 2-inch pieces
- 2 pounds raw shrimp

Fill your largest pot with about 3 quarts of water, dump in the crab boil and bring to a boil. Add sausage and cook 10 minutes. Add corn and cook another 5 minutes. Add the shrimp and cook just until it turns pink, about 2 minutes. Drain and serve with butter for the corn, and the following sauce for the shrimp (or your favorite cocktail sauce.)

Cocktail Sauce

Mix together:

1 cup catsup
Teaspoon or so of creamy horseradish sauce
Splash of lemon juice
Dash or so of Tabasco

This slaw, garnered from Hudson's seafood restaurant in Savannah, can be prepared up to a week in advance of using it.

Seven Day Slaw

1 head cabbage, shredded
1 red onion, shredded
1/3 cup sugar
1 cup vegetable oil
1 cup vinegar
2 tablespoons sugar
1/2 tablespoon dry mustard
1/4 tablespoon salt
1/4 tablespoon black pepper

Toss the cabbage and onion with 1/3 cup sugar. Mix remaining 6 ingredients together in a small saucepan and bring to a boil. Pour boiling mixture over the vegetables, let sit for 5 minutes. Mix well and refrigerate.

Serves 8.

Mike Buckner, who lives with his family in a sort of Eden outside of Junction City, Georgia, gave me permission to use this recipe. Mike operates Fielder's Mill which he inherited from his grandmother, Mrs. Edlow Fielder, or "Miss Ada," as she was affectionately called. There has been a mill in the family in the same location since the 1840s. A dam and a 25-acre mill pond power a water turbine, which runs almost daily, producing corn meal and flour.

The recipe below is for a kind of bread said to have originated in a hunting camp, where the dogs were making too much noise. Someone threw batter into a pot of hot fat, fished out the results and threw it to the dogs, saying "Hush, puppies!"

MISS ADA'S HUSH PUPPIES

1 1/2 cups sifted Fielder's Old Fashioned Corn Meal
3/4 cup self-rising flour
1/4 teaspoon baking soda
1/2 to 3/4 cup finely chopped onion
1/2 teaspoon salt
2 tablespoons sugar
2 eggs
Buttermilk

Mix above ingredients with enough buttermilk to make a stiff batter that will drop from a spoon. Drop by the spoonful into hot grease deep enough to float the batter. When they begin to brown, turn them over. Remove from fat with a slotted spoon. Drain on paper towels placed over brown paper bags.

This recipe came from Hershey, Pennsylvania, where even the local cows eat chocolate. It is leftovers from the Hershey factories, and I'm told the milk they give is wonderful. Well, of course, those cows are contented!

BEST BROWNIES

1/2 cup vegetable oil OR melted butter
1 cup sugar
1 teaspoon vanilla
2 eggs
1/2 cup unsifted all-purpose flour
1/3 cup cocoa
1/4 teaspoon baking powder
1/4 teaspoon salt
1/2 cup chopped nuts, optional

Preheat oven to 350 degrees

Blend oil or butter with sugar and vanilla in a large mixing bowl. Add eggs; beat well, using a spoon. Combine flour, cocoa, baking powder and salt; gradually add to egg mixture. Stir in nuts, if desired.

Spread into a greased 9-inch square pan. Bake for 20 to 25 minutes, or until dough begins to pull away from side of pan. Cool in pan. Cut into squares.

Makes 16 brownies

I have never understood why ice cream makers limit peppermint stick ice cream to the Christmas season. Howard Johnson used to serve it year around. Kinnett makes a great one, and there are one or two other manufacturers making the real thing (i.e., with peppermint stick candy pieces, NOT that green stuff called Mint Chocolate Chip). So we have to make our own in summer. One hot afternoon Lynn and I ate a whole batch of this, although it's supposed to serve as many as 8. It's good, no kidding.

Peppermint Stick Ice Cream

1/2 pound peppermint sticks, about 2 cups crushed
2 cups milk
2 cups cream

Crush peppermint sticks and soak in milk for 12 hours, or until candies are almost dissolved. Stir in the cream and freeze according to ice cream maker directions.

Yields 1 1/2 quarts

This recipe is quite old, clipped from a column by Clementine Paddleford (does anyone else remember her?) and used all these many years with great success.

SIMPLE CHEESE SOUFFLE

1 can Campbell's condensed cheddar cheese soup, undiluted
4 eggs, separated
1/4 teaspoon cream of tartar

Preheat oven to 350 degrees

Heat soup, do not boil. Remove from heat and gradually stir in egg yolks, which have been beaten thoroughly. Beat egg whites with cream of tartar until stiff, but not dry.

Fold soup mixture into egg whites. Turn into an ungreased 1 1/2 quart soufflé dish. Place dish in a roasting pan with 1-inch of hot water. Bake for 1 hour. Serve immediately.

Serves 4.

Early Fall

Friday Dinner

Cocktails
Sunset Caviar

Baked Chicken with 40 Cloves of Garlic
Orange Braised Red Cabbage
Peasant Bread
Chocolate Chip Pie*
Coffee

Saturday Breakfast

Tomato Juice
Broccoli Cheddar Tart
Sliced Mangoes
Coffee

Saturday Lunch

Pimento Cheese Sandwiches*
Gingered Waldorf Salad*
Sweet Potato Chips
Ginger Ale

SATURDAY DINNER

Cocktails
Li'l Smokies with Two Sauces

Black Bean Soup*
Florida Salad
Crusty French Bread
Poached Pears*
Pound Cake*
Coffee

SUNDAY BRUNCH

Cranberry Juice
Sauteed Chicken Livers and Mushrooms
Toast
Cinnamon Apple Slices

Weekend Nibbles — choose a selection from Katie's Cookie Jar.

*Denotes recipe which can be prepared in whole or in part in advance.

Nothing is easier than this appetizer, and yet folks seem to enjoy it as much as more difficult dishes. The great thing is that the makings can be kept in the refrigerator and in the pantry most of the time, in case you need to offer something to drop-in guests.

SUNSET CAVIAR

1 round tin of cream cheese with chives
5 ounce jar of red caviar
Melba Toast rounds

Turn the cream cheese out onto a pretty plate, keeping the shape. Make a small depression in the top and scoop caviar into it. Surround with toast rounds.

Serves 6.

❄ ❄ ❄

If you have oversalted soup, throw in a potato cut in large chunks—you can remove it after a few minutes, or leave it in the soup.

Tomato or V-8 juice makes a good vegetable soup used in place of water.

To soften brown sugar, heat for a minute or two in an open container in the microwave with 1/2 cup water in another container. It will harden again upon cooling.

BAKED CHICKEN WITH 40 CLOVES OF GARLIC

1 tablespoon olive oil
4 pounds of bone-in chicken pieces, skinned
Salt and pepper
40 unpeeled large garlic cloves, about 4 heads
1 3/4 cups dry white wine
4 sprigs fresh thyme OR 1/4 teaspoon dried
1 sprig rosemary OR 1/4 teaspoon dried
2 tablespoons cognac
12 slices peasant bread, toasted lightly

Preheat oven to 350 degrees.

Heat oil over medium heat in a heavy-bottomed flameproof casserole dish wide enough to accommodate the chicken pieces in a single layer. Add chicken, seasoned with salt and pepper. Sauté for 5 minutes, turn and sauté another 5 minutes. (If the bottom of the pan scorches, don't worry. It won't affect the flavor of the dish.) Remove chicken from pan.

Add garlic and sauté, stirring for 3 to 5 minutes, until it is beginning to brown. Spread the cloves evenly in a single layer, and return the chicken to the pan. Add wine, thyme and rosemary; cover tightly, bake for 45 minutes. Check at this point to see if the chicken is tender and fragrant. If not, return to oven for another 15 minutes.

Remove casserole from oven. Heat cognac in a small saucepan and light it with a match. Pour over the chicken and shake the pan until the flame dies. Adjust seasoning.

To serve, place two pieces of the bread on each plate, top one piece with chicken and some of the sauce and several garlic cloves. Guests squeeze out garlic onto the extra slice.

Serves 6.

Orange Braised Red Cabbage

1 large onion, sliced
3/4 stick unsalted butter
3 1/4 to 3 1/2 pounds red cabbage, cored and shredded
1/4 cup sugar
1/2 cup red wine vinegar
1 cup orange juice
1/2 cup dry red wine
1 tablespoon grated orange rind
2 teaspoons salt
6 cloves
1 bay leaf

Preheat oven to 325 degrees.

In a stainless steel pot or enameled casserole, cook the onion in the butter over moderate heat. Salt and pepper to taste and cook, stirring occasionally, until it is translucent. Add the cabbage and cook the mixture over moderately low heat, stirring occasionally, for 5 minutes.

Dissolve the sugar in the vinegar in a small saucepan over moderately high heat. Reduce the mixture to about 3 tablespoons. Add the orange juice and wine and bring to a simmer; pour over the cabbage. Stir in the remaining ingredients. Cover the casserole with a buttered round of foil and then the lid and braise in the oven for 2 hours, stirring once or twice, until the cabbage is tender and has absorbed most of the liquid. Discard bay leaf.

Serves 8.

Rosemary Massengill's restaurant in Columbus served this pie to customers who ordered it over and over. She gave it to me and I pass it on to you. Thanks, Rosemary!

CHOCOLATE CHIP PIE

1 deep dish pie shell, unbaked
5 ounces semi-sweet chocolate chips
1 1/2 sticks margarine
1/2 cup self-rising flour
2 eggs
1 cup sugar
1 teaspoon vanilla

Sprinkle chips in the bottom of the pie crust. Melt margarine and mix in remaining ingredients. Pour this mixture over the chocolate chips.

Bake at 350 degrees for 40 to 45 minutes.

VERY IMPORTANT: Take the pie out of the oven while it is still soft in the center. It will finish cooking after removal.

Serves 6.

I have often found the recipes on the package, or can, or carton to be the best for the product inside. This recipe comes from the side of the Knorr package, and proves the point, I think.

BROCCOLI CHEDDAR TART

1 1/2 cups milk
3 eggs
1 package Knorr's Leek Soup and Dip mix
10 ounce package frozen chopped broccoli, thawed and drained
1 1/2 cups shredded cheddar (OR Swiss or Monterey Jack) cheese
9-inch unbaked deep dish pie crust

Preheat oven to 375 degrees.

In large bowl beat eggs, milk and soup mix together with a wire whisk. Stir in broccoli and cheese; spoon into pie crust.

Bake 40 minutes or until knife inserted into tart comes out clean. Let stand for 10 minutes before serving.

Serves 6.

Every good Southern cook has a pimento cheese recipe. This one is as close as I could come to the Moffett family's recipe, my favorite.

Spicy Pimento Cheese Spread

2 pounds sharp cheddar, grated
3 jars diced pimentos, drained
1 large onion, grated
Parsley flakes
1/2 cup sour cream
1/2 cup mayonnaise
4 cloves garlic, minced
Juice of 1 lemon
Few dashes of Worcestershire sauce
Few dashes of Tabasco
Salt and pepper to taste

Mix all together and refrigerate.

It's amazing how a little ginger can perk up an old favorite. It you toast the nuts in a 250 degree oven for 15 minutes, you'll really wake up the flavor.

GINGERED WALDORF SALAD

2 cups chopped apples
1/2 cup chopped celery
1/4 cup chopped pecans or walnuts
2 tablespoons minced crystallized ginger
1/4 cup golden raisins
2 teaspoons lemon juice
1/2 cup mayonnaise

Mix together first 5 ingredients. Stir together the lemon juice and mayonnaise, then stir into the fruit until it is well coated. Chill until serving time.

Serves 4.

L'il Smokies with Two Sauces

1 pound cocktail sausages

Heat the sausages and serve in a chafing dish or skillet covered with one of the following sauces. Serve with toothpicks.

Bourbon Sauce

Heat together: 1 part catsup
                     1 part bourbon
                     1/2 part brown sugar
until sugar dissolves.

Mustard Sauce

Heat together: 12-ounce jar currant jelly
                     2/3 cup prepared mustard
                     1 medium onion, grated
until jelly is dissolved.

Many recipes for black bean soup call for cooking your own black beans. It's not necessary if you can get hold of several cans of Kirby's black beans. Honestly, I find them as good as home cooked, especially when used in this soup recipe, which is adapted from one published by the Associated Press. I used to buy Kirby's in Miami, and my son brings back a case every time he is in South Florida.

Black Bean Soup

1 large onion, coarsely chopped
2 cloves minced garlic
1 tablespoon olive oil
1/2 cup chopped Canadian bacon or ham
3 16-ounce cans black beans
1 can chicken broth
1 cup carrots cut into 1/8-inch slices
1 large yellow OR red bell pepper, cut into short, thin strips
1 teaspoon cumin
1/2 cup picante sauce
Chopped fresh cilantro, optional

Cook onion and garlic in oil in large saucepan or Dutch oven for 3 minutes; add meat. Cook, stirring frequently, for 1 minute.

Drain and rinse 2 cans of the black beans. Place one can of the drained beans and half the chicken broth in blender and process until smooth. Add pureed beans to saucepan with remaining ingredients (including 3rd can of beans) except cilantro, and bring to a boil. Reduce heat, cover and simmer until carrot is tender 20 to 25 minutes. Ladle into soup bowls, top with cilantro if desired, and serve with additional picante sauce on the side.

Makes 6 cups soup.

Florida Salad

2 ripe avocados, peeled and sliced
2 grapefruits, sectioned
1 can hearts of palm
Fresh or frozen lemon juice
Lettuce leaves
Grapefruit vinaigrette, recipe follows

Place lettuce leaves on four plates. On each, arrange grapefruit and avocado slices alternately, like the spokes of a wheel. Slice the hearts of palm in 1/2-inch rounds and pile in the center of each plate. Drizzle vinaigrette over the salads, and pass extra dressing.

Serves 4.

Grapefruit Vinaigrette

6 tablespoons olive oil
3 tablespoons grapefruit juice
1/4 teaspoon EACH salt, pepper and Dijon mustard
1 clove garlic, peeled

Whisk together the first 5 ingredients, blending well. Slice garlic in half and drop into dressing. Place vinaigrette in covered jar and refrigerate. Before serving, remove garlic and shake well.

Makes about 1/2 cup.

This recipe is from "Susanna Foo Chinese Cuisine" (Chapters Publishing Co.)

Poached Pears with Ginger

1 cup sugar
3 cups water
1 cup white wine
Juice of 1 lemon
2-inch piece of lemon peel
4-inch cinnamon stick
2-inch piece fresh ginger, sliced
3/4 teaspoon anise seeds
6 firm pears

Place first 8 ingredients in a saucepan just large enough to hold all the pears in a single layer. Bring the liquid to a boil, stirring occasionally, and allow to cook about 5 minutes.

Meanwhile, peel and core pears. You can either leave them whole or cut them into halves. Carefully place the pears in the boiling liquid, adding more water if necessary to cover them. Return liquid to a boil; cover the pan and reduce heat to low. Simmer the pears just until they are tender, 10 to 20 minutes, depending on the ripeness of the pears.

Remove the pears from the liquid and set aside. Increase heat to high and boil to reduce the liquid to about 2 cups. Strain the sauce.

If serving hot, place pears in individual serving dishes and spoon sauce over each. If serving cold, place pears and sauce in a serving dish and refrigerate, covered. They will keep for 2 to 3 days.

Serve with raspberry sauce, ice cream, or whipped cream.

Serves 6.

Carolyn and Tom Gates own and operate Gates House Bed and Breakfast and Southern Expressions catering company. Carolyn is an extraordinary cook, and gave me her mother's recipe for pound cake. Judging by this cake, I have a feeling her cooking skills might be inherited.

Edith Alcorn's Pound Cake

1 pound butter
3 cups sugar
6 eggs
4 cups flour
1 teaspoon baking powder
3/4 cup milk
1 teaspoon lemon extract
1 teaspoon vanilla extract

Cream butter well. Add sugar gradually, mixing well. Add eggs, one at a time, beating well after each addition. Sift flour and baking powder together and add alternately with milk. Stir in extracts. Pour into prepared tube pan, and put into a cold oven. Place a cup of water in the oven beside the cake, and turn the oven on to 325 degrees. Bake for 1 hour and 15 minutes, or until the cake tests done. Cool. Remove from pan and ice, if desired, with the following icing.

Icing

1 box confectioner's sugar
3 tablespoons butter
4 tablespoons milk

Heat together. Cool, and drizzle over the pound cake.

Sauteed Chicken Livers and Mushrooms

8 to 10 chicken livers, washed and patted dry
1 large onion, diced
1 tablespoon shortening
6-ounce can sliced mushrooms, drained
Salt and pepper to taste
Paprika to taste
Dash of nutmeg

Heat shortening in a large skillet, add onion and sauté over low heat about 10 minutes. Add mushrooms, mix well, remove all from skillet and place in a bowl.

Add chicken livers to skillet and fry about 3 to 4 minutes on each side. Return onion mixture to skillet, add seasonings, mix well and heat thoroughly before serving on toast points.

Serves 4 or 5.

Late Fall

FRIDAY DINNER

Cocktails
Buffalo Chicken Wings

Pan-fried Trout with Lemon Sherry Glaze
*Baked Stuffed Potatoes**
Baby Blue Salad
Rolls
*Orange Blossom Buttermilk Pie**
Coffee

SATURDAY BREAKFAST

Honeydew Melon Slices
Poached Eggs on English Muffins
Canadian Bacon
*Lemon-Ginger Scones**
Coffee

Saturday Tailgate Lunch

Marinated Tri-color Peppers*
Country Pate*
Purchased Fried Chicken
French Bread
Beer   Wine
Cookies from the Cookie Jar

Saturday Dinner

Cheese Fondue*
Autumn Fruit Compote*
Sparkling Cider
Frozen Pumpkin Squares*
Coffee

Sunday Brunch

Tangerine Juice
Speedy Baked Apples
Fried Corned Beef Hash Patties
Cheese Muffins
Coffee

Weekend Nibbles — choose a selection from Katie's Cookie Jar.

*Denotes recipe which can be prepared in whole or in part in advance.

It is never easy to admit you are wrong about anything.

But I confess I was terribly wrong about Buffalo Wings. I had announced many times that they were "awful, messy, not fit to eat," and held to that opinion until I visited the Anchor Bar in Buffalo, New York. It was there, in this family owned restaurant, that Terressa Bellisimo created Buffalo Wings in 1964.

The family have been serving them ever since, much to their customers' delight.

"Of course," writes Janice Okun of the Buffalo News, *"no restaurateur divulges his best recipe." So she set out to make her own—"spying and tasting like mad." After many, many tries, this is her recipe. In Buffalo, they are always served with celery sticks and blue cheese dressing, she says, and adds, "provide plenty of napkins!"*

BUFFALO CHICKEN WINGS

20 to 25 chicken wings
Vegetable oil for deep-frying
1/4 cup butter
1/2 to 1 bottle (2 1/2 ounces or to taste) Frank's Louisiana hot sauce
Celery Sticks
Blue Cheese Dressing, recipe follows

Cut wings in half. Remove wing tips. Deep-fry wings, about half at a time, in hot oil, until they are crisp and brown, about 10 minutes. Do NOT use any batter or crumbs. Drain wings well.

Melt butter in a saucepan. Add about half the bottle of hot sauce. This will give you medium hot wings. If you like wings hotter, add more hot sauce. If you want them milder, add more butter.

Place wings in a large container with a cover. Pour sauce over wings; mix well.

Serve warm with celery sticks and blue cheese dressing, dipping wings and celery in the dressing as you eat.

Serves 4 to 6.

❄ ❄ ❄

This is Janice Okun's recipe, developed to go with Buffalo Wings, but a great go-with for almost any salad.

BLUE CHEESE DRESSING

2 tablespoons chopped onion
1 clove garlic, minced
1/2 cup fresh chopped parsley
1 cup mayonnaise or salad dressing
1/2 cup sour cream
1 tablespoon lemon juice
1 tablespoon white vinegar
1/4 cup crumbled blue cheese
Salt, pepper and cayenne to taste

Combine onion, garlic, parsley, mayonnaise, sour cream, lemon juice, vinegar and blue cheese in a medium mixing bowl. Season to taste. Chill for an hour or longer before serving.

Makes 2 1/2 cups.

Pan Fried Trout with Lemon Sherry Glaze

For the fish:
- 4 1/2-pound trout fillets
- 3 tablespoons olive oil, divided
- 1 large garlic clove, mashed and minced
- Flour for dredging fish
- Salt and pepper to taste
- 2 tablespoons pecans, chopped fine OR slivered almonds, optional

For the glaze:
- 1/2 cup EACH lemon juice, chicken broth and dry sherry

Sauté half of garlic in 2 tablespoons of the oil in a non-stick pan large enough to hold the fish in one layer. Remove the garlic just before it browns. Add the fillets, which have been dredged in flour and seasoned with the salt and pepper. Cover and cook on medium heat for about 3 minutes per side, depending on the thickness of the fillet. When the fish is fork tender, remove from pan and keep warm in oven while you make the glaze.

Add the rest of the olive oil to pan and sauté the nuts (if desired) and the rest of the garlic until soft. Remove, and add glaze ingredients to pan, increase heat to medium high and allow to reduce, stirring occasionally. This will take a couple of minutes at most.

To serve, place a fillet on each plate, sprinkle garlic and nuts over the top and finish with the glaze.

Serves 4

Baked Stuffed Potatoes

4 medium potatoes, baked
1/2 cup shredded Cheddar cheese
1/3 to 1/2 cup milk
2 tablespoons butter, softened
1 egg, beaten
Salt and pepper to taste
Paprika

Cut a thin slice lengthwise from each potato and scoop out the inside, leaving a thin shell.

Combine potato with cheese, milk, butter, egg, salt and pepper and mash until smooth. Spoon mixture into shell; sprinkle with paprika.*

In a 2 1/2 quart shallow oval dish, arrange potatoes in a circle. Cover with waxed paper. Microwave at medium-high for 4 to 6 minutes. Let stand, uncovered, for 3 minutes.

Serves 4.

*At this point, potatoes may be held, refrigerated, until serving time. Increase heating time by a minute or two.

Baby Blue Salad

9 ounce package baby spinach leaves
4 ounce package crumbled blue cheese
1 can mandarin orange slices
1/2 cup toasted walnut pieces
Grape tomatoes, optional
Balsamic Vinaigrette, recipe follows

Arrange ingredients on salad plates and pass the dressing.

Serves 6.

Balsamic Vinaigrette

1/2 cup balsamic vinegar
3 tablespoons Dijon mustard
3 tablespoons honey
2 large garlic cloves, minced
1/4 teaspoon EACH salt and cider vinegar
1 cup olive oil

Whisk together first 7 ingredients until well blended. Gradually whisk in olive oil, blending well.

Makes 1 2/3 cups.

Here's an old favorite, with new zest—a touch of orange flavoring.

ORANGE BLOSSOM BUTTERMILK PIE

1 pie crust, lightly toasted and cooled
1/2 cup melted butter
2 eggs, beaten
1 cup sugar
1 tablespoon flour
2 tablespoons orange zest
1 teaspoon EACH orange and vanilla extract
1 cup buttermilk
Grated nutmeg

Preheat oven to 350 degrees.

Stir eggs into melted butter; add sugar and sift in flour, mixing thoroughly. Stir in buttermilk, orange zest and extracts. Pour into cooled pie crust. Grate nutmeg generously over the top. Bake 45 to 50 minutes, or until filling is set. Cover pie crust rim during the last 20 minutes to prevent over-browning.

Serves 6.

COOK'S NOTE: If you have not yet gotten a zester, do yourself a favor and get one. I use one called "Microplane."

You already know how to poach eggs, but this little information, clipped from Parade Magazine, *makes it easier to cook more than one.*

How to Poach an Egg

Bring 4 cups of water and 1 tablespoon of white or cider vinegar to a gentle simmer over medium low heat in a large, nonreactive pan.

Break an egg into a cup, and then slip it into the simmering water. It is best not to cook too many eggs at once, as they might stick together. Cook to desired consistency, about 3 to 4 minutes.

Using a slotted spoon, remove the egg and immediately dip it into a bowl of cold water to stop the cooking; then place in a bowl of warm water until you are ready to use the eggs, but no longer than 5 to 10 minutes.

Before serving transfer the eggs to paper towels to drain, then trim away any unsightly strands of egg white.

Serve on toast or English muffins.

If you want to dress the eggs up, sauté pieces of Canadian bacon and place under the eggs on toasted English muffins, and if you like, cover the whole with a cheese or Hollandaise sauce.

Hot buttery scones make any weekend special. Lynn has taken most of the trouble out of these by concocting a dry mix you make before guests arrive. On the morning you serve them, just take out the mix and add the wet ingredients and fruit. However, if you want an easier morning K.P. duty, bake and freeze them days or weeks before your guests arrive—these will freeze beautifully. Just take them out to thaw on the morning you want to serve, pop the foil package into a 325 degree oven until steaming, about 12 to 15 minutes, while you prepare the rest of breakfast.

DO-AHEAD DRY SCONE MIX

2 cups all purpose White Lily flour
1/4 cup sugar
2 1/2 teaspoons baking powder
1/4 teaspoon salt
1/4 cup shortening or margarine
1/4 cup cold butter, cut into about 6 pieces

In a large bowl mix together the dry ingredients and cut in shortening, using a pastry blender or your fingers. When the mixture resembles corn meal, cut in the butter pieces. Stop when the butter has been reduced to the size of English peas.

Pour scone mix into a plastic zip lock bag and refrigerate up to 2 weeks.

For Lemon Ginger Scones, see next page.
For Orange Scones, see page 139.

Lemon Ginger Scones

Preheat oven to 425 degrees.

Take out the scone mix (see preceding page) and pour into a large bowl.

Add to the dry mix:
- 6 tablespoons minced crystallized ginger
- 2 tablespoons minced dried apricots
- Zest of one lemon, chopped*

In a small bowl, blend together
- 1 large egg
- 1/2 cup plain yogurt
- 1/2 teaspoon EACH lemon juice and lemon extract

Pour the liquid into the dry scone mix and stir gently until it begins to hold together, and then turn out onto a well-floured board. With floured hands, fold in half twice and then pat into an 8-inch square about 1 inch high. Neaten the edges. With a very sharp knife dipped into flour, cut the dough into 9 squares (3 across and 3 down.)

Using a spatula dipped in flour, move scones to a baking sheet, placing them 2 inches apart. Brush with a bit of melted butter, sprinkle with sugar. Bake on middle rack for about 15 minutes. (Halfway through baking time, turn pan around for even browning.)

Serve immediately or cool on a rack to room temperature, wrap tightly in foil and freeze for later use.

Yields 9 scones.

*See Cook's Note on page 62.

I believe I clipped this recipe from Cooking Light *magazine several years ago. At any rate, it is a perfectly gorgeous and delicious dish for a summer picnic or tailgate lunch.*

MARINATED TRI-COLOR PEPPERS

2 tablespoons olive oil
1 EACH large red, yellow and green bell pepper, cut into 1/2 inch wide strips
1 large white onion, halved lengthwise and cut into 1/2 inch slices
1/4 cup white wine vinegar
Salt and freshly ground white pepper
2 tablespoons minced fresh basil

Heat oil in heavy large skillet; add peppers and onion strips. Cover and cook until peppers exude liquid and are slightly softened, about 5 minutes. Transfer to a bowl and add vinegar, salt and pepper. Cover and refrigerate until well chilled.

Just before serving, mix basil into the peppers. Serve cold or at room temperature.

Serves 4 to 6.

This is a slightly modified version of Abby Mandel's recipe for a simplified paté. It is wonderful for picnics or a cold summer buffet. Don't tell anyone how easy this was to make—total prep time before baking is about 15 minutes.

COUNTRY PATÉ

2 cloves garlic, peeled
1 small onion, peeled and quartered
1 pound raw, boneless, skinless chicken or turkey breast, cut into 1-inch cubes
1/2 pound premium quality thick bacon, cut into 1-inch pieces
2 chicken livers (about 3 ounces)
2 large eggs
1/4 cup cognac
3/4 teaspoon cinnamon
1 teaspoon salt
1/4 teaspoon EACH grated nutmeg and ground allspice
1/4 pound smoked ham, cut into 1/4-inch dice

Place oven rack in center of oven and heat it to 350 degrees. Butter a 4-cup loaf pan.

In food processor with metal blade running, drop garlic and onion through feed tube and process until finely minced. Add chicken, bacon and livers. Pulse 6 times, then process continuously until smooth, about 1 minute total.

Add eggs, brandy and seasonings. Process 10 seconds, stopping once to scrape down the bowl. Stir in the smoked ham, and spoon into prepared pan. Bang pan a few times on the counter to work out air holes; cover with a piece of buttered aluminum foil. Bake until thermometer registers 160 degrees. This will take about 90 minutes.

Remove from oven and weight down the loaf with a foil-wrapped brick or other heavy object. Let cool to room temperature, then refrigerate until thoroughly chilled.

To serve, loosen loaf from pan with spatula and invert onto serving plate. Slice thin, and garnish with gherkins and radish roses. Serve with a crusty French bread and a variety of mustards.

Makes about 10 slices.

Autumn Fruit Compote

2 Gala apples, peeled and sliced into eighths
1 Anjou pear, peeled and sliced into eighths
3 tablespoons lemon juice
3 tablespoons butter
1/4 cup lemon (or orange) marmalade
3 navel oranges, peeled and cut into sections

Toss apples and pear with lemon juice. Sauté mixture in 2 tablespoons of the butter, turning gently until tender. Transfer with slotted spoon to serving bowl. Add remaining butter and marmalade to pan and cook over medium heat, stirring until marmalade is melted. Pour mixture over fruit, add orange sections and toss gently.

Serves 4.

This elegant dish takes only a few minutes to prepare, especially if you've already grated the cheese, (or bought it already grated) and cubed the bread (which can be held in the refrigerator in plastic bags.) Guests serve themselves, spearing a morsel with a fondue fork, and dipping into the cheese.

SWISS CHEESE FONDUE

2 teaspoons cornstarch
1/4 cup Kirsch or apple brandy
1/2 clove garlic
1 1/2 cups dry white wine
1 pound coarsely grated Swiss cheese
Freshly grated nutmeg and black pepper to taste
2 long baguettes stale French bread, cut into 1-inch cubes
Pint cherry tomatoes
Package Li'l Smokies, or other ready to eat sausage, sliced or cubed

In a small bowl stir together cornstarch and liqueur.
Rub inside of a fondue pot with the garlic. Pour in the wine and heat on moderate flame until you see tiny bubbles forming on the bottom. Stir in the cheese by handfuls, stirring in a zigzag motion until the cheese is melted. Do not let it boil. Stir in the cornstarch mixture; add nutmeg and pepper. Reduce heat to low.

Serves 4 as a main course, 6 to 8 as an appetizer.

NOTE:
The first person to lose a morsel in the fondue has to either
    1. give the next party
        OR
    2. kiss the host

Pam Stacy gave me this recipe about 25 years ago. I've enjoyed serving it ever since. You can keep this easily made, delicious dessert in the freezer a long time if it is properly wrapped—and what a joy it is to have on hand during the holidays.

FROZEN PUMPKIN SQUARES

2 cups (15-ounce can) cooked pumpkin
1 cup sugar
1 teaspoon salt
1 teaspoon EACH ginger and cinnamon
1/2 teaspoon nutmeg
1 cup pecan pieces, toasted in a 325 degree oven for 10 minutes
1/2 gallon vanilla ice cream, softened
36 whole gingersnaps
Whipped cream for garnish, optional
18 pecan halves for garnish, optional

Combine pumpkin, sugar and spices; stir in pecans.
In a chilled bowl, fold pumpkin mixture into softened ice cream.

Butter the bottom of a 9-x-13-inch pan. Line the pan with half the gingersnaps and top with half the ice cream mixture; repeat.

Freeze until firm, about 5 hours. Cut into squares and garnish as desired.

Serves 12.

In microwaving these stuffed apples, you lose nothing but time. If you prepare the stuffing mix in advance, they practically make themselves. During apple season if you keep a batch of the stuffing ingredients in the refrigerator, you'll be able to make quick snacks or, with a topping of vanilla ice cream, desserts.

Speedy Baked Apples

3 tablespoons butter, softened
3 tablespoons firmly packed brown sugar
1 teaspoon EACH ginger and cinnamon
2 tablespoons chopped pecans or walnuts
2 tablespoons golden raisins, chopped
2 tablespoons dried apricots, chopped
4 fresh baking apples
? fresh lemon

Mix together the butter, brown sugar, spices, nuts and dried fruit. (This can be kept in the refrigerator indefinitely.)

Core the apples, leaving the bottom intact, or plugging the bottom with a piece of dried apple. Peel the top thirds of the apples, and squeeze lemon juice over the peeled area. Spoon the filling into the cavities. Arrange the apples in a deep microwaveable dish.

Microwave on high for 8 minutes. Spoon cooking liquid over them and serve.

Serves 4.

Fried Corned Beef Hash Patties

2 15-ounce cans corned beef hash
2 tablespoons butter

Open both ends of the cans, lay them down on a cutting board and push the corned beef hash out, using the edge of the can to make uniform slices. You'll get 5 to 6 patties per can. Melt the butter in a skillet and add the rounds. Brown on both sides and serve.

Serves 6 to 8.

COOK'S NOTE: For another breakfast, use the patties as the base for fried or poached eggs.

Salt and pepper meat just before placing it in a hot oven, and again after removing it from the oven. This will prevent the salt drawing out the juices before the meat is cooked.

When roasting poultry, place the breast end in the back of the oven, because ovens are generally hotter in back, and the bird will cook more evenly.

This recipe came from the Stovall House, a delightful Bed & Breakfast near Sautee, GA.

Cheese Muffins

2 cups flour
1 tablespoon baking powder
2 tablespoons sugar
1/8 teaspoon garlic salt
Dash pepper
1 egg, beaten
1 cup milk
1/4 cup vegetable oil
1 cup grated sharp Cheddar

Mix together dry ingredients and stir in remaining ingredients just until mixed.

Pour batter into muffin pans and bake at 375 degrees until lightly browned.

Makes 24 muffins.

Early Winter

Friday Dinner

Cocktails
Spiced Shrimp*

Turkey Cassoulet*
Red & Orange Salad
French Bread dipped in Olive Oil and Herbs
Sticky Date Pudding with Toffee Sauce
Coffee

Saturday Breakfast

Pineapple Spears
Cheese Toast
Cranberry Bread*
Bacon
Crock Pot Hot Chocolate

Saturday Lunch

Hot Potato Soup
Crackers
Ginger Muffins*
Hot Tea

Saturday Dinner

Cocktails
Cheese Wafers*   *Rosemary Nuts**

Roast Pork Loin with Peach Sauce
Corn Pudding
Sauteed Spinach with Garlic
Chocolate Cherry Bars*

Sunday Brunch

Grapefruit Sections
Huevos Saltillo*
Assorted Sweet Rolls
Coffee

Weekend Nibbles — choose a selection from Katie's Cookie Jar.

*Denotes recipe which can be prepared in whole or in part in advance.

Everyone seems to love boiled shrimp. These are so good as is that cocktail sauce isn't needed. The secret is in steeping the liquid for at least half an hour before adding shrimp.

SPICED SHRIMP

2 to 3 celery tops
1 large onion, quartered
2 tablespoons Worcestershire sauce
6 tablespoons lemon juice
3 tablespoons salt
6 cloves garlic
1 1/2 teaspoons black peppercorns
1 1/2 teaspoons whole allspice
1 crushed bay leaf
1 teaspoon crushed red pepper
1/2 teaspoon whole cloves
1 quart beer
1 1/2 pounds fresh shrimp, heads removed

Simmer all ingredients except shrimp for 30 minutes.
Raise heat to a boil and add shrimp. Cook just a couple of minutes until the shrimp turn red. Drain immediately in a colander. Serve hot, or chilled, with lemon wedges.

Serves 6 as an appetizer, 3 to 4 as an entrée.

My brother-in-law George sends me a wonderful smoked turkey every Christmas.

I save enough of it, frozen in cubes, to make this dish. You can use plain turkey or chicken, but try to get the smoked—it makes a difference. And use a good quality of sausage. This dish is the result of tinkering a bit with a recipe that appeared in Merle Ellis' column, "The Butcher."

TURKEY CASSOULET

1 1/2 to 2 pounds leftover smoked turkey, cut into 2-inch cubes
1 medium onion, chopped
2 tablespoons butter
1 to 2 cups chicken broth
1 bay leaf
1/2 teaspoon salt
1/2 teaspoon thyme
2 pounds canned white beans, drained
1/2 cup tomato paste
1/2 to 3/4 pounds smoked sausage, cut into 1-inch slices

Preheat oven to 350 degrees.

In a large sauté pan, cook the onion in butter until soft and translucent. Add a cup of the broth, the bay leaf, salt, thyme and beans to the pan. Stir in the tomato paste and mix well. Stir in the turkey and sausage and turn into a 2 1/2 quart oven to table casserole dish.

Cover and bake for 20 minutes; uncover, adding a bit more chicken stock, and bake for an additional 10 to 15 minutes until hot and bubbly.

Serves 6.

Orange and Red Salad

Lettuce leaves for lining plates
4 navel oranges
2 red onions
French dressing, recipe follows

Peel and slice oranges, arrange on 4 plates lined with lettuce leaves. Slice red onions thinly and arrange on top of oranges. Drizzle with dressing.

Serves 4.

French Dressing

6 tablespoons olive oil
2 tablespoons red wine vinegar
1/2 teaspoon salt
1/4 teaspoon pepper
1/4 teaspoon dry mustard

Whisk all together, place in lidded cruet and chill. Shake well before serving.

Yields about 1/2 cup.

On a visit to Canada's Prince Edward Island, home of that favorite fictional character Anne of Green Gables, we visited Dalvay by the sea. This elegant inn serves wonderful food in a magnificent country setting. Every food writer in our group loved this dessert. You will too.

STICKY DATE PUDDING WITH TOFFEE SAUCE

1 3/4 cups packed pitted dates (about 10 ounces)
2 cups water
1 1/2 teaspoons baking soda
2 cups all-purpose flour
1/2 teaspoon EACH baking powder, ginger and salt
6 tablespoons butter, softened
1 cup sugar
3 large eggs
Toffee Sauce (recipe follows)

Preheat oven to 375 degrees. Butter and flour an 8-inch square baking pan 2 inches deep, knocking out excess flour.

Coarsely chop dates and simmer them in the water for 5 minutes, uncovered. Remove pan from heat and stir in baking soda. Let mixture stand for 20 minutes.

Meanwhile, sift together flour, baking powder, ginger and salt. In a large bowl, beat sugar and butter until light and fluffy. Beat in eggs thoroughly, one at a time. Add flour mixture in 3 batches, beating until just combined after each addition. Add date mixture and stir in with a wooden spoon until well combined. Pour batter into pan set in larger baking pan. Add enough hot water to larger pan to reach halfway up sides of smaller pan. Bake 35 to 40 minutes, or until a tester comes out clean. Remove small pan of pudding to cool on a rack until warm. Cut into squares, ladle on warm sauce and top with vanilla ice cream, if desired.

Serves 6 to 8.

Toffee Sauce

1 3/4 sticks butter
1 1/3 cup packed light brown sugar
1 cup heavy cream
1/2 teaspoon vanilla

Melt butter in a heavy saucepan over moderate heat; add brown sugar and bring mixture to a boil, stirring occasionally. Stir in cream and vanilla and simmer, stirring occasionally until thickened slightly, about 5 minutes.

"Non-cooks think it's silly to invest two hours work in two minutes enjoyment; but if cooking is evanescent, so is the ballet."

Julia Childs

My mother didn't learn to cook much but fudge until I was 13, but she made up for lost time later. This is one of her recipes I particularly like—it's easy, inexpensive and good.

LOUISE TENNENT'S CRANBERRY BREAD

4 tablespoons butter
2 cups sugar
2 eggs
1 teaspoon EACH salt and soda
4 cups flour
1 1/2 cups orange juice
2 cups halved cranberries
1 cup nuts, cut small

Preheat oven to 350 degrees.

Cream butter and sugar, mix in eggs one at a time. Sift dry ingredients together and add alternately with orange juice. Stir in nuts and cranberries. Bake in greased loaf pans for 1 hour or until a tester comes out clean.

Makes 2 loaves.

Crock Pot Hot Chocolate

4 cups water
3/8 cup sugar
4 cups milk
1/2 cup chocolate syrup
1/4 teaspoon salt

Heat water and pour into crock pot. Add sugar and salt and stir until dissolved. Stir in milk and chocolate syrup, cover and turn on high for half an hour. Turn below medium for serving. Top with marshmallows or whipped cream.

Makes 2 quarts.

This is quite a versatile recipe: It is a hearty cold weather soup, or can also be used to make vichyssoise.

Potato Soup

3 cups peeled potatoes, thinly sliced
3 cups leeks or onions, thinly sliced
1 1/2 quarts chicken stock
1/2 to 1 cup cream
Salt and pepper to taste
4 tablespoons butter
2 to 3 tablespoons minced chives, for garnish

Put potatoes and onion into pot with chicken broth. Season with salt and pepper and bring to a boil. Turn down to low and partially cover. Simmer 40 to 50 minutes, or until vegetables are tender. Pour in small batches into food processor or blender and puree.

Return to pot and add butter and cream. Heat through but do not boil. Garnish with chives.

Serves 6.

Vichysoisse

Follow potato soup recipe through pureeing. Add cream but not butter. Over salt.

Chill, adding cream as needed to achieve consistency to your taste. Sprinkle with chives.

This sweet muffin recipe of Lynn Willoughby's tastes like warm gingerbread and is a hit at breakfast, lunch or tea. The batter keeps in the refrigerator for up to a month, so you can make these hot treats with only a moment's notice. If you're expecting a big crowd, the recipe doubles easily.

REFRIGERATOR GINGER MUFFINS

10 tablespoons vegetable shortening
1/2 cup sugar
2 eggs
1/4 cup unsulfured molasses
1/4 cup honey
2 cups plain flour
1/2 teaspoon salt
1 teaspoon soda
1 teaspoon ground ginger
1/8 teaspoon ground cinnamon
1/8 teaspoon ground allspice
1/2 cup buttermilk

Cream together the shortening and sugar. Add eggs one at a time, beating well after each addition. Add molasses and honey and beat well. Sift flour with soda and spices. Add flour and buttermilk alternately.

Store in tight-lidded plastic container in refrigerator and use whenever you like.

TO BAKE: Preheat oven to 425 degrees. Fill greased muffin tins slightly over half full.

Place in oven and set timer for 4 minutes. Reduce heat to 375 and continue to bake for another 8 or 9 minutes until tester comes out clean.

I have never liked squeezing dough out of a cookie press, so this is my version of cheese straws.

CHEESE WAFERS

1/4 pound butter, cut into chunks
1/2 pound sharp cheese, grated
1 1/2 cups all-purpose flour
1 teaspoon salt
1/2 teaspoon Worcestershire sauce
1/2 teaspoon cayenne pepper
Pecan halves, about 36, optional

Allow butter and cheese to come to room temperature. Place them in bowl of a food processor and pulse to blend. Stir in all remaining ingredients except pecans and process briefly until it makes a dough.

Refrigerate until the dough is easy to handle, and then shape into a log a little wider than a quarter. Wrap in plastic and refrigerate overnight.

Preheat oven to 325 degrees. Slice cheese log into 1/4-inch wafers, top each with a pecan half, if desired, and bake for 10 to 12 minutes.

Yields about 3 dozen.

May be stored in an airtight container for a week.

Susi Hamlett, "The canape queen," gave me this recipe. They can be made in advance, but hide them from the family or there won't be any left for the guests.

Rosemary Nuts

2 cups mixed nuts (walnuts, pecans, almonds, etc. – no peanuts)
2 1/2 tablespoons butter
2 tablespoons fresh rosemary
1 teaspoon salt
1/2 teaspoon cayenne pepper

Melt butter and toss with nuts and seasonings. Bake on a cookie sheet in a 350 degree oven for 10 minutes.

Watch carefully, and toss once to redistribute nuts.

Take a half hour or so one day to walk through your grocery store without a shopping list or a shopping cart. Go up and down the aisles and really look. You are sure to find at least one or two items to fascinate you, and perhaps, be useful in your kitchen.

This recipe was provided at a luncheon sponsored by the Georgia Peach Commission.

Pork Loin Roast

1 cup soy sauce
2 tablespoons lemon juice
1 tablespoon minced garlic
2 tablespoons minced fresh or 2 teaspoons dried tarragon
2 tablespoons minced fresh or 2 teaspoons dried basil
3 to 4 pounds pork tenderloin

In a gallon-sized zip-lock bag, combine all ingredients except pork; seal and shake to blend. Add roast and marinate in refrigerator overnight (or at least 5 hours), turning occasionally.

Preheat oven to 325 degrees. Remove pork from marinade and place in a shallow roasting pan. Roast for 2 to 3 hours, basting with reserved marinade every 30 minutes, until meat thermometer inserted into thickest part registers 160 degrees for medium or 170 for well done. Let stand for 15 minutes, tented with foil, to make slicing easy.

Serve with peach sauce.

Serves 8.

Peach Sauce

12 ounce jar peach preserves
10 ounce jar apple jelly
4 tablespoons Dijon mustard
1 tablespoon prepared horseradish

Mix all ingredients well, cover and store in refrigerator. Makes about 1 1/2 cups.

Stella Burns Butler, my neighbor in the North Carolina mountains, gave me this delicious corn pudding recipe. The ingredients can be kept on hand for a quick fix.

CORN PUDDING

15 ounce can creamed corn
15 ounce can corn niblets, drained
1 box Jiffy corn muffin mix
2 eggs, beaten
3/4 stick melted butter
8 ounces sour cream
1 cup grated sharp cheddar

Preheat oven to 350 degrees.

Mix first six ingredients. Pour into a Pyrex baking dish and sprinkle with the cheese. Bake 40 to 50 minutes, or until the center is set.

Serves 6 to 8.

COOK'S NOTE: For a southwestern touch, stir in a 4.5 ounce can of chopped green chilies, drained, and 1/4 teaspoon ground cumin.

Sauteed Spinach with Garlic

2 (10-ounce) packages frozen leaf spinach
3 cloves minced garlic
3 tablespoons olive oil
Salt to taste
Lemon juice to taste

Defrost spinach and squeeze dry.

Sauté garlic in olive oil a minute or two; add spinach. Cook, stirring, until the spinach is hot and incorporated with the oil and garlic. Season to taste with salt and lemon juice.

Serves 6.

The gathering of friends and relatives marks all the milestones of a lifetime, from christening celebration to final good-bye. At each of these, the sharing of food makes a connection among us. A dish brought to a sick friend, the celebration of holidays and graduations and weddings — whether events are glad or sad, the sharing of food brings us together.

This recipe was a winner in the Pillsbury Bake-Off many years ago, and has been a family favorite ever since, prepared for my son's birthday every year.

CHOCOLATE CHERRY BARS

1 package Pillsbury Fudge Cake mix
21-ounce can cherry pie filling
1 teaspoon almond extract
2 eggs, beaten

Preheat oven to 350 degrees. Using solid shortening, not oil, grease and flour a 13-x-9-inch baking pan. Combine ingredients, stirring by hand until well mixed; pour into prepared pan. Bake 25 to 30 minutes, or until tester comes out clean. While bars cool, prepare frosting, and pour over partially cooled bars.

FROSTING

1 cup sugar
5 tablespoons butter
1/3 cup milk
6 ounces semi-sweet chocolate pieces

Combine sugar, butter and milk in a small saucepan. Boil, stirring constantly, for 1 minute. Remove from heat, stir in chocolate pieces until smooth.

Susi Hamlett gave us this version of the "prepare it the night before and cook it in the morning" strata type dish.

HUEVOS SALTILLO

20 ounce loaf good bread (sourdough, Italian, etc.)
2 cups mild picante sauce
1 pound bulk sausage, crumbled, cooked and drained
6 ounce can chopped green chilies
1 pound shredded cheddar
6 eggs, beaten
3 cups whole milk

Butter a 9-x-13-inch pan and place a layer of bread on the bottom. Scatter half the cheese, sausage and picante sauce over the bread; put all the chilies over this. Repeat the layer of bread, cheese, sausage and picante sauce.

Mix the eggs and milk and pour over all. Refrigerate overnight.

Next morning, bake at 350 degrees until browned lightly on top, about 50 minutes.

Additional cheese and sauce may be put on top, and dish returned to the oven for 5 minutes. Let stand 15 minutes before serving.

Serves 8.

Late Winter

Friday Dinner

Cocktails
Light Hummus with Pita*

Chicken Tchakhbelli*
Packaged Yellow Rice
Steamed Broccoli
Sweet Potato Pie*
Coffee

Saturday Breakfast

Cheesy Beef on English Muffins*
Curried Fruit
Coffee

Saturday Lunch

Minestrone*
Crackers

SATURDAY DINNER

Cocktails
*Hot Sausage Balls**

Pasta Putenesca
*Tossed Salad with Raspberry-Horseradish Dressing**
Garlic Bread
*Cherry Shortcake on Orange Scones**
Coffee

SUNDAY BRUNCH

Tangerine Juice
Country Ham
Grits Casserole
Scrambled Eggs
*Basil Cream Biscuits**
Coffee

Weekend Nibbles — choose a selection from Katie's Cookie Jar.

*Denotes recipe which can be prepared in whole or in part in advance.

Light Hummus

2 cloves garlic
2 15-ounce cans garbanzo beans, drained and rinsed
5 tablespoons lemon juice
1 tablespoon sesame oil
2 teaspoons olive oil
1/2 teaspoon ground cumin
1/8 teaspoon ground allspice
Salt and cayenne pepper to taste
1/2 cup plain low-fat yogurt

With machine running, drop garlic down feed tube of a food processor until finely minced, a few seconds. Add beans, lemon juice, oils and spices and process into a rough puree. Add yogurt and process with a few more pulses until smooth.

Refrigerate up to 2 days before serving with crackers, pita bread or raw vegetables.

This is a strange name for a wonderful do-ahead dish; clipped so long ago I don't remember where it's from or what it means. However, it's a favorite because it's good, and you can make it ahead, refrigerate and then bake later.

CHICKEN TCHAKHOKHBELLI

2 fryers, skinned and cut into pieces
1/4 pound butter
2 large onions, sliced
3/4 cup sherry
1/2 cup tomato juice
1 large can mushrooms
8 ounces tomato sauce
2 teaspoons paprika
1 teaspoon salt
1/2 teaspoon sugar
1 cup hot chicken stock
Pepper to taste

Sauté chicken in butter until browned; remove to a baking pan. Sauté onion in frying pan fats until yellow. Add other ingredients and bring to a boil. Pour sauce over chicken.
(At this point you can refrigerate the dish and bake it later.)

Preheat oven to 400 degrees. Bake chicken dish 30 minutes. Turn chicken pieces and bake another 30 minutes. Serve with yellow rice.

Serves 6 to 8.

Old time Columbusites will remember when there was a Kirven's department store downtown. And will probably also remember fondly the Kirven's Tea Room, and its delicacies. This recipe is adapted from the one served there.

KIRVEN'S TEA ROOM SWEET POTATO PIE

4 large sweet potatoes, cooked and mashed
2 sticks butter, melted
2 cups sugar
4 eggs
1 teaspoon pumpkin pie OR apple pie spice
2 tablespoons lemon juice
1 small can evaporated milk
1 teaspoon vanilla
2 9-inch pie shells

Stir butter into sweet potatoes, add sugar. Add eggs one at a time, stirring well.

Mix in remaining ingredients, beating well. Pour into pie shells, and bake for 15 minutes at 450 degrees. Lower oven temperature to 350 degrees and bake another 45 minutes, or until pies are set. Cover crust rims with foil to prevent over browning.

Makes 2 pies.

The great thing about this dish is that, if you freeze some chopped onion and green bell pepper in little packets, this is practically an instant breakfast.

CHEESY BEEF ON ENGLISH MUFFINS

1 small onion, finely chopped
1/2 green bell pepper, finely chopped
2 tablespoons butter
1 package Stouffer's creamed chipped beef
1/2 cup milk
1/2 cup grated cheddar cheese
2 English muffins, split and toasted

In medium-sized saucepan, sauté onion and bell pepper in butter until soft. Add frozen chipped beef and milk, stirring until all is incorporated. Stir in cheese until melted.

Serve over muffin halves.

Serves 4.

Variations of this recipe were de rigueur for brunch in the '60s, and for good reason. It seems everyone loves this comfort food.

CURRIED FRUIT

3 large cans fruit (pineapple, peaches, pears and/or cherries)
3/4 cup light brown sugar
1/2 cup melted butter
2 teaspoons curry powder, or to taste

Drain the fruit and pour into a large, shallow baking pan. Stir butter, sugar and curry together; pour over the fruit and bake at 300 degrees for about an hour.

Serves 6 to 8.

Kissin' don't last —
Cookin' do!

This hearty soup is perfect for a winter lunch. It can be made the day before serving and reheated—actually improving the taste.

MINESTRONE

4 slices bacon, chopped
1/4 cup chopped onion
1/2 cup chopped carrots
1 cup sliced zucchini
1 clove garlic, minced
15.5 ounce can cannellini beans
15.5 ounce can chick peas
1/2 cup fresh or frozen peas
1 can niblets corn
1 can diced tomatoes
1 package frozen chopped spinach
3 beef bouillon cubes
6 cups water
Seasonings to taste: Salt, pepper, Italian spices, etc.

Sauté bacon until brown, drain and reserve.

Sauté next 4 ingredients lightly in 1 tablespoon of the bacon grease. Add rest of the ingredients, except bacon, bring to a boil and simmer 10 minutes.

Just before serving, top with crumbled bacon.

A favorite on Southern tables, this appetizer can be frozen until needed, and disappears from the plate in short order.

SAUSAGE BALLS

1 pound hot pork sausage
2 cups grated sharp cheese
3 cups Bisquick mix

Mix ingredients well. Roll into small balls; mash with a fork on cookie sheet to flatten.

At this point you can freeze them or bake at 400 degrees for 10 to 12 minutes. Make these small and bake until good and brown.

Makes about 7 dozen.

RASPBERRY–HORSERADISH SALAD DRESSING

8 ounces Ken's Steakhouse Raspberry-Walnut Oil Vinaigrette
1 to 1 1/2 teaspoons creamy horseradish sauce

Shake together in a cruet or dish with a tight-fitting lid.

Jim Moffett loved this dish. On his 70th birthday, we enjoyed it in Rome at a little restaurant on the Via Veneto.

Pasta Putenesca

2 to 3 tablespoons olive oil
6 garlic cloves, slivered
1 tablespoon red pepper flakes
10 anchovies, minced (optional)
28-ounce can diced tomatoes
3 tablespoons capers
1/2 cup Calamata olives, sliced (optional)
Chopped parsley for garnish
1 pound angel hair pasta, cooked and drained

In a heavy skillet, sauté garlic, red pepper flakes and, if desired, anchovies, for about 10 minutes. Add tomatoes, capers and, if desired, olives, and cook for 5 minutes more.

Add spaghetti to sauce and mix well. Top with freshly grated Parmesan cheese and chopped parsley.

Serves 4.

Lynn and I were playing with the concept of cherry shortcake one afternoon at Big Ridge in North Carolina when we came up with this recipe, which we think is darn good. We hope you will think so too. At any rate, it's a great Winter-Valentine dessert.

CHERRY SHORTCAKE

2 14.5-ounce can pitted red tart pie cherries in water
1 cup juice, drained from cans
6 tablespoons sugar
1/2 teaspoon almond extract
1/4 cup cold water mixed with 2 tablespoons cornstarch
Whipped cream for garnish
6 orange scones, recipe follows on next page

Drain cherries, reserving juice. Place one cup of reserved juice in saucepan, stir in sugar and heat until sugar is dissolved. Dissolve cornstarch in the cold water, mix into sweetened juice and stir constantly over low heat until liquid is clear and thickens. Stir in almond extract and then cherries.

Split scones. Spoon some of mixture onto bottom half; add scone top and another spoonful of cherries. Top with a dollop of whipped cream.

Serves 6.

Orange Scones

In advance, put together the dry scone mix found on page 97. To this, add

Zest of 1 orange
1/8 teaspoon nutmeg

In a small bowl, mix together

1 large egg
1/2 cup plain yogurt
1/2 teaspoon orange extract

Pour the liquid ingredients into the dry and stir gently to combine. Just as it begins to hold together, turn out onto a well-floured board. With floured hands, fold the dough in half twice and then pat into an 8-inch square about an inch high. Neaten the edges.

With a very sharp knife dipped in flour, cut the dough into 9 squares (3 across, 3 down.) Using a spatula dipped in flour, move scones to a baking sheet, a couple of inches apart. Brush with a bit of melted butter, sprinkle with granulated sugar.

Bake in 400 degree oven for 15 minutes, turning pan halfway through baking time.

These freeze well. If not using immediately, cool them on a rack to room temperature, wrap tightly in foil and freeze. To serve, put the foil package into a 325 degree oven for about 12-15 minutes.

Makes 9 scones.

COOK'S NOTE: The secret to perfect scones is to handle the dough as little as possible.

Country Ham and Red-Eye Gravy

1 package country ham pieces labeled "Biscuit Slices" allowing about 2 ounces a person
4 tablespoons butter or margarine
1/4 cup black coffee
1/2 cup water

Place ham slices in a skillet and cover with about an inch of water. Heat until just steaming. Pour off the water, and add butter to the pan. Heat on medium setting to melt butter and brown meat on both sides (about 3 minutes.) Remove ham to a serving plate and keep warm.

Add coffee and water to pan, bring to a boil and scrape pan to release browned bits.

Serve over grits or biscuits.

Serves 4 to 6.

These biscuits are melt-in-your-mouth tender and really easy to make if you use a food processor. They can be served hot or cold, and are especially good filled with slivers of ham.

BASIL CREAM BISCUITS

1/2 cup loosely packed basil leaves
2 cups self-rising flour
Pinch of salt
3/4 cup heavy cream
2 tablespoons melted butter

Preheat oven to 425 degrees.

Process basil leaves for 6 to 8 seconds until chopped fine. Add flour and salt, and scrape down sides of bowl. With motor running, pour cream directly through the open feed tube. Process just long enough to incorporate the cream. Take dough out and knead a few times to incorporate the flour. If you still have a lot of dry flour, add 1 tablespoon more cream. Roll out to 1/4-inch thickness. Cut into 2-inch diameter circles. Dip both sides of each biscuit in melted butter. Place on ungreased baking sheet and bake 10 minutes.

In not used immediately, may be stored in an airtight container, served cold or reheated in oven in foil.

Yields about 3 dozen biscuits.

HAND METHOD: Chop basil fine and in a roomy bowl add flour and salt; stir. Stir in cream. Knead dough a few times, and proceed as above.

Isabelle Swift Ferrell was a friend in college and is now a summer neighbor in North Carolina. She serves this dish there.

QUICK GRITS CASSEROLE

1 cup grits
5 cups liquid (half milk, half water)
1 teaspoon salt
1 tablespoon sugar
1/4 cup butter
1/2 pound sharp cheddar, grated
4 eggs, beaten

Cook first 4 ingredients for 5 minutes. Remove from heat and add butter and cheese. Stir in eggs. pour into a greased casserole and bake at 350 degrees for about an hour.

Serves 8.

Katie's Cookie Jar

Fill a cookie jar with one of the treats below for weekend nibbler.

We promise they will disappear fast.

Awesome Oatmeal Cookies 145

Choco-Macs 146

Classic Peanut Butter + Cookies 147

Maple Snaps 148

Mocha Chip Cookies 149

Oops! Cookies 150

Pecan Shortbread 151

Scotch Rangers......................................152

You will note in these recipes that Katie does not skimp on ingredients—that's what makes these cookies so good. Each recipe will make a lot of cookies, and they do not divide well, but they do freeze well. When you have time, make the dough, form the cookies and freeze them individually, taking out only what you need. Just think: You can have cookies warm from the oven at the drop of a hat!

Here's the technique: Place wax paper on a cookie sheet, lay the formed cookies on the sheet, cover in plastic wrap to prevent freezer burn, and freeze. Put the frozen individual cookies in a Ziploc freezer bag. Double bag if they are to be frozen for a while. No need to do anything different with the frozen cookies except to add a minute or two to the baking time.

Awesome Oatmeal Cookies

2 cups all purpose flour
1/2 teaspoon salt
1 teaspoon baking powder
1/2 teaspoon baking soda
2 1/2 teaspoons ground cinnamon
1/2 teaspoon ground allspice
1 1/3 cup butter
1 cup granulated sugar
1 cup brown sugar
2 large eggs
1 generous teaspoon vanilla
2 tablespoons orange juice
1 cup raisins
1 cup chopped pecans OR walnuts
2 1/2 cups quick oats

In a bowl, whisk together first 6 ingredients and set them aside.

In a large separate bowl, cream together the butter and the sugars. Beat the eggs in one at a time. Add the vanilla and the juice and mix until well blended. Add the dry ingredients to the wet in small batches. Add in the oatmeal, raisins and nuts and mix for 4 to 5 minutes until thoroughly combined.

Roll into 1-inch balls and place on an ungreased cookie sheet about 2 inches apart. Flatten them slightly.

Bake at 350 degrees for 13 to 15 minutes.

Makes 5 dozen.

Choco-Macs

3 1/2 cups all purpose flour
3/4 teaspoon baking soda
2 cups unsalted butter
3 teaspoons vanilla
1 1/2 cups granulated sugar
1 1/2 cups brown sugar
2 large eggs
1 cup powdered cocoa
1/4 cup heavy cream
1 cup macadamia nuts
1 cup semi-sweet chocolate chips
1 cup white chocolate chips

Whisk together flour and soda and set aside.

Cream butter and sugars well, add vanilla. Add eggs one at a time. Add cocoa and cream, scraping sides of bowl often, and mix until creamy and fluffy. Add flour mixture, blending until just mixed.

Fold in nuts and chips all at once.

Drop by spoonfuls onto an ungreased cookie sheet and bake at 325 degrees for 15 to 18 minutes. Let cool before removing from cookie sheet.

Makes about 3 dozen good-sized cookies.

Classic Peanut Butter + Cookies

1 cup unsalted butter
1 cup peanut butter
1 cup granulated sugar
1 cup brown sugar
2 large eggs
2 cups all purpose flour
1 teaspoon vanilla
1 teaspoon baking soda
1 cup peanut butter chips

Cream butter and peanut butter together. Add sugars in slowly and cream all together, stopping frequently to scrape down the bowl. When well creamed, add eggs one at a time.

Whisk together dry ingredients in a separate bowl. Add in small batches to the creamed mixture with mixer on low. Mix in chips by hand.

Roll the batter into a log about 1 1/2 inches in diameter. Cut into 1/2 inch thick slices and place about 2 inches apart on an ungreased cookie sheet.

Bake at 325 degrees for about 15 minutes.

Makes 5 dozen.

Maple Snaps

1 cup granulated sugar
1 cup brown sugar
1 1/2 cups unsalted butter
2 large eggs, beaten
1/2 cup real maple syrup
1 teaspoon cinnamon
1 teaspoon ground cloves
1/2 teaspoon freshly grated nutmeg
1 teaspoon salt
3 teaspoons baking soda
4 1/2 cups all purpose flour
Raw sugar, to roll cookies in

Cream together the sugars and butter, add the eggs. Add the maple syrup and beat until very light and fluffy.

Whisk together all of the dry ingredients; add slowly to the wet and mix completely. Refrigerate dough for an hour or so to make forming the cookies easier.

Roll into 1 inch balls, roll balls in the raw sugar and place on an ungreased cookie sheet.

Bake at 350 degrees for 10 to 12 minutes.

Makes 4 to 5 dozen.

COOK'S NOTE: This dough can be refrigerated for up to a week before baking.

Mocha Chip Cookies

1 cup milk chocolate chips
1 cup softened unsalted butter
1 cup brown sugar
1 cup granulated sugar
2 large eggs
2 tablespoons instant espresso in 2 teaspoons hot water
2 tablespoons plus 1 teaspoon Kahlua
2 teaspoons vanilla
3 cups flour
1 1/2 teaspoons baking soda
1/2 teaspoon salt
1 package semi-sweet mini chocolate chips

Melt the milk chocolate slowly over low heat, stirring often, and set aside.

In a large bowl, cream butter and sugars. Add eggs one at a time and mix until very smooth. Mix in the espresso, Kahlua and vanilla. Add the melted chocolate and let your mixer run while you whisk together the dry ingredients. Gradually add the dry with the wet ingredients, then stir in the semi-sweet chocolate chips.

Refrigerate the dough while the oven heats to 350 degrees.

Form the cool dough into 1 inch balls (handling as little as possible) and place on an ungreased cookie sheet about an inch apart. Bake for just 8 to 10 minutes. Take them out when they have started to spread and are getting crackly on top. (You can bake them longer if you like a crispy cookie, but they are great warm and chewy.)

Makes 2 dozen.

Katie named these cookies when she was making several batches of cookies at once and got confused about which recipe was which. She finally just said "What the heck" and mixed together the batter for two different kinds. It made some great cookies.

OOPS! COOKIES

2 cups butter
1 cup chunky peanut butter
1 1/2 cups brown sugar
1 cup granulated sugar
3 eggs, beaten
5 cups rolled oats
3 cups flour
2 teaspoons baking soda
1 teaspoon salt
2 teaspoons cinnamon
1 package chocolate chips OR 1/2 bag chocolate and 1/2 bag peanut butter chips

Cream first four ingredients together. Add eggs and mix.

Whisk together next five ingredients. Add dry to wet ingredients slowly, then stir in chips. Drop by spoonfuls onto ungreased cookie sheets.

Bake at 325 degrees for 12 to 15 minutes.

Makes 5 to 6 dozen

COOK'S NOTE: This recipe does not reduce well, but it does freeze well.

See notes beginning "Katie's Cookie Jar" for the technique.

Pecan Shortbread Cookies

1 cup butter
1/2 cup confectioner's sugar
1/4 teaspoon salt
1 teaspoon vanilla
2 3/4 cups plus 2 tablespoons all purpose flour
1/4 cup pecans ground until fine as flour

Beat the butter until light and fluffy; slowly add the sugar and then the salt and vanilla. Decrease mixer speed and gradually add flour and ground pecans.

Divide the dough in half, roll into 2 logs about 1 1/2 inches in diameter. Refrigerate them while the oven heats to 325 degrees.

Slice into 1/4-inch slices and place on an ungreased cookie sheet. Prick each slightly with a fork. For an extra fillip, you can make an indentation on the top of these cookies and put a little apple butter or a bit of your favorite jam in the indentation. Or press a pecan on the top.

Bake for about 15 minutes

Makes 2 dozen.

COOK'S NOTE: This dough may also be rolled out to 1/4-inch thickness and cut with a cookie cutter.

Scotch Rangers

1 cup unsalted butter
1 cup brown sugar
1 cup granulated sugar
2 large eggs, beaten
1 teaspoon vanilla
2 cups plain flour
2 cups quick (NOT instant) oats
1/2 teaspoon baking powder
1 teaspoon baking soda
1/2 teaspoon salt
1 cup flaked coconut
1 cup butterscotch chips

Cream butter and sugars until light and fluffy. Add eggs and vanilla. Whisk together dry ingredients with coconut and stir into dough by hand. Mix in chips.

Roll a teaspoonful of dough into a ball, place on ungreased cookie sheets at least two inches apart—they spread!

Bake at 350 degrees until golden, about 10 to 12 minutes. Be careful not to overcook. Remove at once to rack to cool.

Makes 3 dozen.

COOK'S NOTE: For a basic ranger recipe, leave out the butter scotch chips.

Index

Apples, baked, 104
Asparagus, pan roasted, 18
Aspic, tomato, 18
Baby Blue Salad, 94
Beef
    Brisket, 42
    Cheesy, 133
    Rib Roast, 59
Biscuits
    Basil Cream, 141
    Cheddar, 36
Black Bean Soup, 82
Blintz, Ricotta, 20
Blueberry French Toast, 45
Bread
    Cranberry, 115
    Lemon, 62
Broccoli
    And Mushrooms en croute, 10
    Cheese Tart, 78
    Salad, 33
Brownies, 68
Buffalo Wings, 90
Buttermilk Orange Pie, 95
Cake
    Chocolate Torta, 27
    Pound, 85
Carrot-Ginger Soup, 63
Cauliflower, Tangy Zapped, 60
Caviar
    Mushroom, 24
    Sunset, 74
Cheese
    Blue Dressing, 91
    Biscuits, 36
    Crock o', 48
    Fondue, 102
    Goat Cheese Tarts, 57

    Muffins, 106
    Pimento, 79
    Souffle, 70
    Wafers, 119
Cherry Shortcake, 138
Chicken
    Picante, 32
    Roasted with Garlic, 75
    Salad, curried, 46
    Tchakhbelli, 131
    Wings, 90
Chicken Livers & Mushrooms, 86
Chocolate
    Cherry Bars, 124
    Chip Pie, 77
    Hot, Crock Pot, 116
    Torta, 27
Corn
    On the cob, 48
    Pudding, 122
Corned Beef Hash Patties, 105
Cranberry Bread, 115
Cucumber Soup, 29
Curry
    Curry Accompaniments, 26
    Fruit, 134
    Shrimp, 25
Date Pudding, 113
Eggs
    Baked Swiss, 28
    Huevos Saltilla, 125
    Poached, 96
Fish
    Flounder Fillets, 17
    Trout, Pan Fried, 92
Florida Salad, 83
Flounder Fillets, Zapped, 17
Four Spices, 41
Fondue, Cheese, 102
French Dressing, 112

French Toast
    Blueberry, 45
    Peach Upside-down, 15
Fruit
    Apples, Baked Stuffed, 104
    Autumn Compote, 101
    Burton, 51
    Curried, 134
Gingered
    Lemonade, 47
    Waldorf Salad, 80
Goat Cheese Tarts, 57
Golden Coins, 35
Green Beans, Marinated, 52
Grits Casserole, 142
Ham, Country, 140
Hash, Corned Beef Patties, 105
Hummus, 130
Hush Puppies, 67
Ice Cream
    Pie, 50
    Peppermint Stick, 69
Jalapeno Bites, 17
Jezebel Sauce, 64
Lamb Roasted a la Grecque, 11
Lemon
    Bread, 62
    Ginger Lemonade, 47
    Pie, 19
Li'l Smokies with sauces, 81
Low Country Boil, 65
Minestrone, 135
Muffins,
    Cheese, 106
    Ginger, 118
Mushroom Caviar, 24
Nuts, Rosemary, 120
Onions
    Vidalia Casserole, 49
    Yum-Yum Appetizer, 31

Orange & Red Salad, 112
Pasta Putanesca, 137
Pate
    Chicken Liver, 40
    Country, 100
Pea Salad, 61
Peach
    Cobbler, 44
    French Toast, 15
Pears, Poached, 84
Peppermint Ice Cream, 69
Peppers, Marinated Tri-color, 99
Pie
    Buttermilk Orange, 95
    Chocolate Chip, 77
    Ice Cream, 50
    Lemon, 19
    Strawberry, 34
    Sweet Potato, 132
    Tomato, 52
Pimento Cheese, 79
Pork Loin Roast, 121
Potatoes
    Golden Coins, 35
    Soup, 117
    Stuffed Baked, 93
Pound Cake, 85
Pudding, Sticky Date, 113
Pumpkin Squares, Frozen, 103
Raspberry Sauce, 50
Red Cabbage, Braised, 76
Red Rice Salad, 12
Ricotta Blintz Casserole, 20
Salads
    Aspic, Tomato, 18
    Baby Blue, 94
    Broccoli, 33
    Curried Chicken, 46
    Florida, 83
    Green Bean, 52

    Orange & Red, 112
    Pea, 61
    Peppers, Marinated Tri-color, 99
    Red Rice, 12
    Roasted Vegetable, 43
    Slaw, Seven Day, 66
    Shrimp, 16
    Waldorf, Gingered, 80
Salad Dressings
    Balsamic Vinaigrette, 94
    Blue Cheese, 91
    French, 112
    Grapefruit Vinaigrette, 83
    Raspberry-Horseradish, 136
Sangria, 56
Sauces
    Bourbon, 81
    Cocktail, 65
    Mustard, 81
    Peach, 121
    Raspberry, 50
    Toffee, 114
Sausage
    Balls, 136
    Wraps, 51
Scones
    Lemon Ginger, 98
    Mix, 97
    Orange, 139
Shrimp
    Curry, 25
    Low Country Boil, 65
    Salad, 16
    Spiced, 110
Slaw, Seven Day, 66
Soufflé, Cheese, 70
Soup
    Black Bean, 82
    Carrot Ginger, 63
    Cucumber, 29

    Minestrone, 135
    Potato, 117
    Vichyssoise, 117
Spinach, Sauteed with Garlic, 123
Squash Casserole, 13
Strawberry Pie, 34
Summer Pudding, 14
Sweet Potatoes
    Golden Coins, 35
    Pie, 132
Tea, Iced Mint, 64
Tomato
    Aspic, 18
    Pie, 52
    Preserves, 58
Torta, Chocolate, 27
Tortilla Rolls, 30
Trout, Pan Fried, 92
Turkey Cassoulet, 111
Vegetables, Oven Roasted, 43
Wafers, Cheese, 119
Waldorf Salad, Gingered, 80

To order additional copies of *Wonderful Weekends*, please fill out coupon below and send with a check or money order for $20.00 plus $3.50 postage and handling for each book to:

WONDERFUL WEEKENDS
P.O. Box 1194
Columbus, GA 31902

Please mail _____ copies of your Cookbook @ $20.00 plus $3.50 postage and handling per book order.

Name: _____

Address: _____

City, State, Zip _____

To order additional copies of *Wonderful Weekends*, please fill out coupon below and send with a check or money order for $20.00 plus $3.50 postage and handling for each book to:

WONDERFUL WEEKENDS
P.O. Box 1194
Columbus, GA 31902

Please mail _____ copies of your Cookbook @ $20.00 plus $3.50 postage and handling per book order.

Name: _____

Address: _____

City, State, Zip _____